A handbook for naturalists

# A handbook for naturalists

edited by
Mark R. D. Seaward

assisted by Susan Joy
and Frank H. Brightman

foreword by
H.R.H. The Duke of Edinburgh

published in association with
Council for Nature/Council for Environmental Conservation
Constable London

First published in Great Britain 1981 by
Constable and Company Limited
10 Orange Street London WC2H 7EG
Copyright © Council for Environmental Conservation
ISBN 0 09 462390 2

Filmset in Monophoto Times New Roman
and printed in Great Britain by
BAS Printers Limited,
Over Wallop, Hampshire

# Foreword
H.R.H. The Duke of Edinburgh

One of the notable characteristics of the British from the earliest times has been their interest in nature. In pictures, books and diaries, and in gardens, parks and forests both amateurs and professionals have left a remarkable record of their enthusiasm in their own native land as well as in all the countries of the old Empire. It is not altogether surprising therefore that they were also the first to notice the ravages of pollution brought on by industrial and urban development, and to initiate what has become a world movement for the conservation of nature.

While this movement had no difficulty gaining wide popular support, it also triggered off a growing interest in the more particular study of various aspects of natural history. I hope this book will prove a great help to all those whose interest in, and concern for, the natural environment has been aroused and who would like to go a stage further to improve their knowledge or to make a practical contribution to the conservation of nature.

1979

# Acknowledgements

I am especially grateful to His Royal Highness The Duke of Edinburgh for contributing the Foreword, and we are all appreciative of his active interest in the work of the Council for Nature since its formation in 1958, until its closure, and transfer of functions to the Council for Environmental Conservation in January 1980.

I gratefully acknowledge the generous help I have received from many persons in the preparation of this book, in particular from my assistant editors, Susan Joy (Secretary of the Council for Nature) and Frank Brightman (Education Officer, British Museum (Natural History)), and the contributors of the various chapters.

Special mention should also be made of the help given by Melinda Appleby (former Secretary of the Council for Nature), Jack Parsons (Chairman of the Council for Nature's Youth Committee), Vanessa Hinton, Andrew Pierssene and Philip Shaw in many aspects of the work.

For the illustrations, I would like to thank: Miss Claire E. Appleby (illustrations 32, 35, 36, 37); Mr Jonathan Joy (illustrations 31 & 33); Mr David Joy (illustration 38).

Illustration 7 is reproduced by kind permission of Macmillan and is taken from M. Ashby (1969) *Introduction to plant ecology*.

My sincere thanks are also due to the publishers for their courtesy and care in seeing the book through to publication.

Mark R. D. Seaward
Bradford, September 1980

# Contents

# List of Contributors

MELINDA J. APPLEBY New Agricultural Landscape Project Officer for Suffolk. (Former Secretary of the Council for Nature.)

FRANK H. BRIGHTMAN Department of Public Services, British Museum (Natural History), London.

BRUCE CAMPBELL Natural history adviser to *The Countryman* magazine. Formerly Head of the BBC Natural History Unit.

HENRY DISNEY Warden and Director of Studies, Malham Tarn Field Centre, Yorkshire.

PAUL HARDING Biological Records Centre, Institute of Terrestrial Ecology.

DAVID HAWKSWORTH Commonwealth Mycological Institute, Kew.

JOHN HEATH Biological Records Centre, Institute of Terrestrial Ecology.

SUSAN M. JOY Executive Officer, Council for Environmental Conservation. (Former Secretary of the Council for Nature.)

PETER PROSSER Headmaster, Cranborne County Middle School, Dorset.

TIM S. SANDS Joint Assistant Secretary, Society for the Promotion of Nature Conservation, Lincoln.

MARK R. D. SEAWARD Senior Lecturer, School of Environmental Science, University of Bradford.

MARTIN SPRAY Senior Lecturer, Department of Landscape Architecture, Gloucestershire College of Art and Design.

JOHN STIDWORTHY Department of Public Services, British Museum (Natural History), London.

# Illustrations

# Preface

*Knowledge is of two kinds. We know a subject ourselves, or we know where we can find information upon it.*

Samuel Johnson (1709–1784)

The study of natural history is not restricted to any particular age group, nor is it only the province of professional biologists. With increasing leisure and mobility, more people than ever before are searching for pursuits to absorb their energies and fill their leisure time profitably. Stimulated by the media, especially by wildlife programmes on radio and television, people of all ages have been encouraged to enquire more deeply into the natural environment about them. The study of natural history is not only highly enjoyable but it can also give the added satisfaction of contributing to scientific knowledge: for example, many major scientific enquiries, such as the various national recording schemes (see Chapter 4), rely heavily on observations made by amateur naturalists.

This book aims to provide practical help for those taking up natural history fieldwork for the first time. It is a successor to the Council for Nature's two previous publications, *Advice for Young Naturalists* (compiled by M. R. D. Seaward, 1965; revised 1969) and *A Handbook for Naturalists* (edited by Winwood Reade and R. M. Stuttard, 1968). Whereas these books were primarily aimed at the young naturalist, this work is directed at a wider audience, as it is felt that today's beginner will include all age groups from the junior enthusiast to the senior citizen taking up a hobby in retirement. This book should therefore prove useful to people attending field courses and extra-mural classes on the subject for the first time, and to those engaged in a variety of teaching situations.

Following an historical survey of British natural history studies (Chapter 1), there is a review of major habitats in Britain (Chapter 2). A guide to essential field equipment, ideas for field projects and guidance on accurate recording of data in the field (Chapter 3) form the next section of the book. Ways in which local recording can be incorporated into national schemes are given in Chapter 4. The facilities provided for the naturalist by field centres and museums are described in Chapters 5 and 6, and the value of zoos and nature trails is considered in Chapters 7 and 8.

It is important for the naturalist to understand the relevant sections of the law, and how to make the best use of the various provisions contained in it to safeguard British wildlife; for this reason particular attention is given to this topic (Chapter 9). Effective preservation of the British fauna and flora is, in the last resort, the responsibility of the individual, and we hope that this book will help to some extent in fostering appreciation of, and promoting the need for, conservation.

Chapter 10 lists the more important societies catering for the naturalist, and indicates the scope of their activities. This list is by no means definitive, since it concentrates on the national organizations that have relatively permanent addresses. Many societies, particularly local or regional ones, have addresses which vary with every change of secretary and it is impractical to include them in this book; in such instances we recommend that enquiries for details of societies catering for a particular interest should be made in the first instance to the nearest museum or library. If this proves fruitless, then CoEnCo (see p. 159) should be able to provide the necessary information.

Guides to the identification of plants and animals found in Britain are fundamental to the work of the naturalist, and we have attempted to provide as comprehensive a list as possible of the major taxonomic works (Chapter 11) that are relevant. This list should be used in conjunction with the ecological references which are quoted at the end of Chapter 2. Inevitably, some of these references will quickly become out of date, but we hope that we have been sufficiently wide ranging in our selection of material to ensure that the list will remain useful for some years to come. We strongly recommend readers to keep abreast of new developments by reading the periodical literature (see p. 172) for a selection of journal titles).

The use of some technical terms is unavoidable: these have been pruned to a minimum, and it is hoped that the meaning of those unfamiliar words which remain will be clear from the text. Furthermore, glossaries are to be found in many ecological and taxonomic works, and there are various biological dictionaries on the market (see p. 171 for a selection). The inclusion of a glossary was thought unnecessary for these reasons.

Mark R. D. Seaward
Bradford, 1979

## The Country Code

The Countryside Commission have prepared the Country Code as a guide to visitors, some of whom are perhaps unaccustomed to country ways. Please remember and observe the following standards of good manners when you go to enjoy the beauties and the pleasures of the garden that is Britain's countryside:

1  **Guard against all risks of fire**

2  **Fasten all gates**

3  **Keep dogs under proper control**

4  **Keep to the paths across farm land**

5  **Avoid damaging fences, hedges and walls**

6  **Leave no litter**

7  **Safeguard water supplies**

8  **Protect wild life, plants and trees**

9  **Go carefully on country roads**

10  **Respect the life of the countryside**

# 1. Natural history in Britain: historical background

Bruce Campbell

British and Irish interest in natural history derives from two ancient sources: interest in animals from the lore of the hunter and crop protector, and in plants from the search by apothecaries and doctors for herbs of medical value. By the sixteenth century the religious, allegorical and fabulous ingredients of the medieval bestiaries were no longer generally accepted. Our knowledge of the wildlife that existed up to this period is gleaned from archaeological evidence, from contemporary writings and accurate observations by literary figures, and from inventories, estate records and church or monastic documents.

A representative naturalist of the sixteenth century is **William Turner** (1508–68), Dean of Wells, often called the father of British ornithology, but whose great achievement was a herbal containing 238 first records of British plants. Exile for his religious beliefs gave him the opportunity to study abroad, where the thirst for knowledge was fast eroding respect for the old authorities. Turner himself was not able to discard all the venerable dross but he did set an example of observation in the field, particularly during his Northumbrian boyhood. Gerard's (1545–1612) *Herbal* is much better known than Turner's but was adapted from a Flemish work. The best zoological work before 1660 was Thomas Penny's (*c.* 1530–1588) *Theatrum Insectorum*.

The Restoration in 1660 saw a great step forward in scientific enquiry. This was partly due to the foundation in London of the **Royal Society**: its formation was a product of more settled times and provided the opportunity for a few pioneers, admittedly mainly of comfortable status, to speculate and even do some fieldwork. At the same time, the opening up of the New World and the Far East brought a stream of plant and animal specimens to Europe and made the need for identification and classification urgent.

**John Ray** (1627–1705) stands out as the great figure of this period; like William Turner he suffered for his beliefs and turned his voluntary exile to good account. His enormous energy and diligence transformed knowledge of most branches of natural history. Stimulated by the problem of the 'fossil record', Ray began to ask the sort of question that eventually toppled Archbishop Ussher's chronology (which set the Creation in 4004 BC), but like other enlightened contemporaries he found it difficult to shake off the chains of the past entirely. For instance, William Harvey, discoverer of the circulation of the blood, believed in spontaneous generation, while Sir Thomas Browne, the author of *Religio Medici*, found it hard to understand that the sun did not go around the earth.

Ray's *Cambridge Catalogue* is the first of a distinguished line of county floras; some scarce plants still grow where he knew them. The less well-known **Dr Robert Plot** (1640–1696), produced another prototype, *The natural history of Oxfordshire* (1677), in which he comments on the lack of snakes in the northern part of the county; this remains true and suggests that man's activities are not necessarily always to blame for scarcities.

During the eighteenth century the means to support the great discoveries that were being made by voyagers both in the physical and mental realms were coming into existence—museums, botanic gardens, herbaria, reference books and libraries. Enthusiasts, still overwhelmingly amateur, were forming societies, often of a limited life, at whose meetings they discussed their finds. With the publication of *Species Plantarum* in 1753 and of the tenth edition of *Systema Naturae* in 1758 by the Swedish naturalist **Carl Linnaeus** (1707–1788) came the binomial system of naming plants and animals which is still used today, although in Linnaeus' time of course it lacked an evolutionary or genetic basis.

**Gilbert White** (1720–1793) therefore had a fair basis on which to start. The third, after Turner and Ray, of the clerical founding fathers of British natural history, White owes his unique status to his powers of observation in the field, his concise and graphic style and the fact that, unlike Ray, he wrote in English. White's *The natural history and antiquities of Selborne* (1789) is now the fourth most published book in the English language, and this simple chronicle of his observations in the Hampshire parish, of which he was curate, continues to inspire naturalists all over the world.

White was not, as we would say today, a conservationist. He took part as a young man in the sporting pastimes of the day—hunting, shooting and fishing—'with almost ferocious vigour' as a recent editor has put it. Although White lamented the destruction of birds

1. The naturalist as notetaker. A page from Linnaeus's notebook on his Lapland journey, *Iter Laponicum*

of prey, he probably did not consider that they might become extinct. On the other hand, in his feeling for the living plant or animal he anticipated an attitude which was to grow in strength in the next two centuries.

The honour of being the first protectors of British wildlife in the modern sense goes to two country squires, the Yorkshireman **Charles Waterton** (1787–1865) and **J. F. M. Dovaston** (1782–1854) of Shropshire. Waterton is by far the better known, largely because of the book he wrote on his South American adventures. He forbade his gamekeepers to shoot 'vermin' on his estates, and he put up nestboxes and devised other artificial nesting sites. Dovaston was one of the first men to realize the existence of animal territories.

David Elliston Allen's *The naturalist in Britain* (1976) is essential reading for anyone interested in the development of all branches of the subject in the nineteenth century. A major interest during the early part of the century was the study of geology. As Allen points out it was promoted no doubt by the appointment in 1804 of **Robert Jameson** (1774–1854) to the chair of natural history at Edinburgh where he founded a school of mineralogy modelled on the German one at which he had studied. Geology had economic implications and so the subject was able to attract government money for surveys, although the Geological Society of London, formed in 1807, had no immediate industrial aims.

The theoretical study of geology raised awkward questions as to the age of the earth. Amid various rival views, some plausible and some absurd, the date was pushed quietly farther and farther back. A century after Linnaeus introduced order to biological naming, papers by **Charles Darwin** (1809–1882) and **Alfred Russel Wallace** (1823–1913) were communicated to the Linnean Society of London, promulgating the theory of evolution by natural selection.

It was not until the publication of Darwin's *The origin of species* in 1859, however, that the main controversy over evolution was really sparked off. The appearance of this book was one of the outstanding events in the history of British natural sciences and a landmark in the development of human thought. No doubt the ferment of the Darwinian era, allied to the increasing affluence and leisure for more people, helped the rise of local societies (though the oldest, the Ashmolean Natural History Society of Oxfordshire, claims lineage back to 1828), as well as of national bodies devoted to the specialist branches of the subject; the **British Ornithologists' Union**, for instance, was founded in 1858.

By the end of the nineteenth century the main fact-finding and recording machinery, more or less as we know it now, had been set up; and all over the country amateur naturalists, in the unsuitable clothing of the time, went on excursions not unlike those their descendants enjoy today. Interest in the seashore, particularly in rock pools, was a great feature of mid-Victorian social life.

This new public was an obvious target for books of all kinds, from magnificently illustrated volumes, such as the botanical works of the Sowerby family and John Gould's bird books, to moral tales for children by well-intentioned authors to whom the name of Darwin was anathema. The natural history societies began

2. Engraving of a heron from Gilbert White's *Natural history of Selborne*

publishing their own journals, proceedings and transactions, though magazines produced on a purely commercial basis tended to have the same precarious life as their successors today.

Before the 1850s were over, the camera's potential for portraying nature had been realized. In 1888 **Benjamin Wyles** of Southport succeeded in photographing gulls in flight; but pioneer nature photography will always be associated with the brothers **Richard** (1862–1928) and **Cherry Kearton** (1871–1940), the one concentrating on Britain, the other following the trail to Africa.

One aspect of the increasing organization of natural history which causes trouble today (and even more so since local government reorganization) is its consolidation on a county basis. British counties, cutting across watersheds and at one time full of small enclaves, have little to commend themselves as boundaries for naturalists. The botanist **H. C. Watson** (1804–1881) divided the British Isles into 112 vice-counties, which made a little more sense, and the scheme was generally followed for plant distribution studies and to a lesser extent by zoologists. (See Appendix A.) In Scotland **J. A. Harvie-Brown** (1844–1916) and his colleagues devised 'faunal areas', usually delimited by watersheds, and published a series of *Vertebrate faunas* based on them.

The idea was not taken up south of the border until the **Wildfowl Trust** adopted broad regions for its studies of British and Irish ducks, geese and swans. The Trust's wildfowl counts each winter, which began in 1948–49, are the longest running study of any group of animals and a highly organized example of the co-operative technique for collecting records; through the International Wildfowl Bureau they have been copied in many other countries and there are now two international counts each season.

The germ of network recording may be found in Gilbert White's circle of correspondents exchanging information. The Anglo-Irish **A. G. More** (1830–1895) attempted an enquiry into status on a national scale in 1865; his questionnaire forms are preserved at Oxford.

In modern times the *Atlas of the British flora* (1962, revised 1976), was an outstanding achievement after ten years' fieldwork by members of the Botanical Society of the British Isles. As dot distribution maps on the National Grid 10 km squares, the data were processed by the Biological Records Centre (BRC), then Nature Conservancy, of the Monks Wood Experimental Station (see Chapter 4). After fieldwork from 1968 to 1972, *The atlas of breeding birds in Britain and Ireland* (1976) was produced by the British Trust for Ornithology with the help of the BRC and was based on 285 000 records from some 10 000 observers. The BRC has also promoted distributional studies of other vertebrates and of the larger invertebrates. It has actively encouraged the setting up of regional record centres in several museums, so that the amateur observer need not feel that his observations are lost to science; modern information retrieval methods ensure their survival and availability.

Another important development during the past century has been the appearance not only of professional biologists in museums and laboratories, but in the field too. There has always been a tendency among professionals to leave fieldwork to the amateur; there have been, however, outstanding exceptions, like **Edward Forbes** (1815–1854), a brilliant all-round naturalist who made many expeditions, but died six months after his appointment as Professor of Natural History at Edinburgh.

The ecological approach was pioneered in Britain by two Scots, the Smith brothers, who were influenced by studies at Montpellier University. **William Smith** (1866–1928) became a lecturer at Leeds and some of the first field studies of British vegetation were made on the moors of Yorkshire. A local committee of the Yorkshire Naturalists' Union led to the British Vegetation Committee, which in 1913 became the **British Ecological Society** and soon afterwards admitted zoologists as well.

The outstanding ecological survey of the early twentieth century was that organized by **R. Lloyd Praeger** (1865–1953) on Clare Island in Galway Bay from 1911 to 1915 with an interdisciplinary team that produced 68 reports. There are two other notable dates in this period: the formation in 1912 of the **Society for the Promotion of Nature Reserves** (now the Society for the Promotion of Nature Conservation), founded by Lord Rothschild, and in 1914 the first Act to protect any mammal—namely the grey seal, of which over half the world population breeds round the coasts of Britain and Ireland.

In 1869 an Act was passed to prevent the massacre of birds on

3. T. H. Huxley, one of the great Victorian naturalists – a drawing from *The Graphic*
1883

Yorkshire cliffs. This legislation was not motivated purely for the
protection of the wildlife interest, but rather to curtail the number of
shipwrecks which had formerly been prevented by the carrying noise
of the birds in bad weather.

This law was as difficult to operate effectively as most subsequent
laws have proved. Twenty years later was formed what became in
1904 the **Royal Society for the Protection of Birds. W. H. Hudson**
(1841–1922) wrote on its behalf and left the royalties on his books to
the society, which had from its earliest days a strong interest in
education though it was originally formed by a group of ladies to
fight the use of bird plumage in millinery.

Apart from work by museums, bird study up to 1914 remained
predominantly amateur. On the scientific side came the first bird-

ringing schemes in 1909 and the foundation of the journal *British Birds* in 1907. Early contributors to this publication were the brothers C. J. and W. B. Alexander who, by quantifying their observations, brought a scientific approach to bird-watching.

Many countries were ahead of Britain in the provision of National Parks and Nature Reserves, and the years between the two world wars were very disappointing. Only in Norfolk, where the National Trust owned the coastal terneries at Blakeney and Scolt Head, was progress made. In 1926, through the determination of a small group led by Dr S. H. Long, was formed the **Norfolk Naturalists' Trust**, with power to acquire and lease land. This remained the only active body for 20 years.

In 1920 Professor **James Ritchie** published *The influence of man on animal life in Scotland*, and in 1932 his former student **Colin Matheson** wrote *Changes in the fauna of Wales within historic times*—two works which at least prepared the stage for a new attitude. In 1921 **T. A. Coward** (1867–1933) gave an address in Manchester (subsequently published), which presented an almost modern conservation ethic to an apparently deaf generation. But not quite deaf: men like **Charles Elton** and **E. M. Nicholson**, who led the natural history movement after 1945, were coming to the fore. Elton's **Bureau of Animal Population**, the **British Trust for Ornithology**, inspired by Nicholson and B. W. Tucker, and the publication of *The British Isles and their vegetation* (1939) by **A. G. Tansley**, were hopeful signs in a troubled decade.

An enormous surge of interest in natural history was evident after the Second World War simultaneous with the emergence of a movement concerned with the wider implications of nature conservation. Nature conservation is concerned with the need to balance man's activities with his environment and the management of valuable habitats to maintain diversity so that the survival of wildlife is ensured. Nature conservation cannot really be separated from resource management whether for food, forestry, sport or any other needs of man.

The members of both the new natural history and nature conservation movements came from all sorts of backgrounds, differing socially and in their interests. Societies started up again with booming membership; books, including those illustrated by the fruits of new photographic techniques, were avidly collected; natural history and wildlife conservation programmes became firmly established on radio; the Collins' 'New Naturalist Series' of titles expressed the mood of the times. The moment was ripe for statutory action to match this enthusiasm.

## Government agencies

A series of committees, official and unofficial, had in fact been at work for many years, trying to adapt the national park concept, so successful in the wide open spaces of the USA and Africa, to the relatively small-scale landscape of Britain and post-war construction had sparked off more efforts. The whole complicated story has been set forth in John Sheail's *Nature in trust* (1976).

It is sufficient here to note that a government White Paper was published in 1947 which led in 1949 to the creation of **National Parks** and the designation of **Areas of Outstanding Natural Beauty** in England and Wales, with a Commission to look after them, and a **Nature Conservancy** for the whole of Britain, with powers to buy, lease and enter into management agreements for reserves. Sir **Arthur Tansley** (1871–1955), the leading plant ecologist, appropriately became the Nature Conservancy's first Chairman. The Conservancy could advise local authorities who wished to use their new powers to declare local reserves, it could establish wildfowl refuges and field stations for biological research and it could also give grants and contracts to students, universities and other bodies for the same purpose.

Since 1949 the governmental picture, in terms of ministries and their functions, has been subject to many changes. In 1973 the Nature Conservancy's duties were divided, the main element emerging as the Nature Conservancy Council, responsible to the **Department of the Environment**, itself hardly a gleam in Whitehall's eye 20 years before. The new Council is concerned primarily with the management of **National Nature Reserves**, the designation of **Sites of Special Scientific Interest** and with advising other government agencies and local authorities about nature conservation matters; it can make grants, commission necessary research and do some research of its own.

The main research function and the field stations of the former

Nature Conservancy have now passed to the **Institute of Terrestrial Ecology**, itself part of the **Natural Environment Research Council** and responsible to the Department of Education and Science. The Nature Conservancy Council now operates the Bird Protection Acts and other Acts of Parliament protecting wildlife, formerly the province of the Home Office.

The **Home Office**, since it controls the police, can be involved in prosecutions under the Deer Act (1963), the Badgers Act (1973) and the Conservation of Wild Creatures and Wild Plants Act (1975). The **Ministry of Agriculture, Fisheries and Food** has an infestation control branch, which pursues much good ecological research though it sometimes falls foul of naturalists over such controversial matters as the control of oystercatchers in respect of their depredations on cockle fisheries. It also has the unenviable task of dealing with transmission of bovine tuberculosis by badgers.

The **Forestry Commission** owns several million acres and manages the largest potential nature reserve in the country. This nature reserve is now run on an enlightened 'multiple use' basis: 'coniferization' of traditional hardwood areas has ceased and, although there is still opposition to the planting of conifers on bare hillsides, it is difficult to see how else the Commission can discharge its function of building up the 'national forest' without taking good agricultural land. In January 1978 the otter was added to the creatures protected under the 1975 Act but only in England and Wales. Soon afterwards the Forestry Commission declared all its Scottish holdings a sanctuary for otters, a most imaginative gesture by a government agency.

The **Central Electricity Generating Board** sets up educational nature reserves in the surrounds of its generating stations and tries to minimize the effect of its activities within the landscape by sympathetic planting schemes. The new **Water Authorities** have a responsibility to conserve the wildlife along our rivers and to maintain water quality by controlling pollution levels. Also involved with the natural scene and its inhabitants are the **Countryside Commission for England and Wales**, which succeeded the National Parks Commission in 1968, and the **Countryside Commission for Scotland** established in 1967, but the main emphasis of their activities is on the provision of recreational facilities and the enhancement of the landscape.

In addition to these government agencies the independent, but privileged (in so far as the land they own is alienable) **National Trust** and **National Trust for Scotland** are both important landowners, controlling such famous sanctuaries as the Farne Islands and St Kilda. Although regarded primarily as the custodians of great houses and lovely gardens, both these organizations consider wildlife interests in the management of their properties.

In the purely voluntary field the Society for the Promotion of Nature Reserves, whose founding in 1912 has been mentioned, had acquired several small but important reserves by 1939. In the post-war era it emerged as the original promoter of the Council for Nature in 1958 and as the umbrella body for the **Nature Conservation Trusts**. After the lead by the Norfolk Naturalists' Trust (page 27), Trusts were started up in Yorkshire (1946) and Lincolnshire (1948); then the pace quickened until by 1964 the whole of England and Wales was covered by Trusts, some combining several counties. Scotland has its own **Wildlife Trust**, which is concerned with the conservation of all forms of wildlife in Scotland. More recently the **Ulster Trust for Nature Conservation** has been established in Northern Ireland.

The Nature Conservation Trusts are distinct from natural history societies (although the Pembrokeshire Bird Protection Society, after a period as the West Wales Field Society, turned itself into the West Wales Trust) and attract a somewhat different membership. The Society for the Promotion of Nature Reserves, already regarded as the Trusts' own association, was granted a new charter in 1976 and became the **Society for the Promotion of Nature Conservation** (SPNC) with offices at Nettleham in Lincolnshire.

The Trusts between them now have some 1 100 reserves covering 32 400 ha (80 000 acres). At a county level they work with the local authority, particularly with respect to planning and education, with the Regional Officers of the Nature Conservancy Council, with other government agencies where appropriate, with the agents of the National Trust, the branches of the Council for the Protection of Rural England and Wales, and with natural history societies.

As a landowning voluntary body, the **Royal Society for the Protection of Birds** (RSPB) shares many problems with the Nature

Conservation Trusts. It owns or leases some of the best bird sanctuaries in Britain and its membership has leapt up in recent years to about a quarter of a million, reflecting our concern for birds since they are one of the most obviously beautiful and vulnerable groups of our wildlife. Although the interests of the birds come first, all forms of wildlife are protected on RSPB reserves which, as far as possible, the society is taking into the security of ownership.

The specialist societies, both national and local, many of them now more than a century old, continue to increase and develop. An overlap between the membership of committees usually ensures harmony between local societies and the Nature Conservation Trusts; the acquisition and management of nature reserves by the latter often involves the help of the specialist societies. Conferences and meetings, reports and newsletters keep the naturalists of Britain in touch with each other and preserve that relationship between amateur and professional which other countries envy.

In 1943 the Council for the Promotion of Field Studies, later the **Field Studies Council**, was set up, to be followed in 1945 by the similar **Scottish Field Studies Association**. Their centres cater primarily for college and university students, sixth form pupils and the amateur naturalist. The Field Studies Council's lead has been followed by the establishment of facilities at youth hostels, by courses at bird observatories and by the setting up of field centres in the wilder parts of Britain by universities and local authorities and by organizations such as the Brathay Trust, which is also much concerned with expeditions overseas. Linked with the 'adventure' theme, but primarily with scientific objectives, these centres are one of the developments in British education most encouraging to the naturalist.

Adopting a more informal approach are the **Young Ornithologists' Club** of the RSPB, the **Wildlife Youth Service** of the World Wildlife Fund and the '**WATCH**' club of SPNC. Working through schools, local groups or individuals, these clubs now count their members in thousands.

The rapid growth of local and national societies resulted in an awareness of the need to have a single body to represent the interests of natural history and wildlife conservation, and in 1958 the **Council for Nature** was formed (closed December 1979). It co-ordinated the views of its twelve constituent bodies which included the leading wildlife conservation organizations and the learned societies of Great Britain. On their behalf the Council made representations to the Government and other relevant authorities. It also had a duty to keep natural history and nature conservation matters before the public which it did through its comprehensive publication *habitat* (now published by CoEnCo) and a central information office. It maintained a strong interest in youth work and was the umbrella body for some 300 affiliated natural history societies.

Because of its diverse functions the Council for Nature had initiated many activities over its 21 years of existence, including the organization of the National Nature Weeks of 1963 and 1966, and *The Countryside in 1970* Conference. Later on it concentrated primarily on its forum role at a national and international level through its membership of a number of important committees which included the **Council for Environmental Conservation** (CoEnCo) (see p. 159) and the **European Environmental Bureau** (EEB). This latter organization is the only body recognized by the European Economic Community for consultation on environmental matters with the voluntary sector. The Council for Nature also advised the All Party Parliamentary Conservation Committee which still encourages Members of Parliament to take an interest in environmental matters.

One of the most important projects initiated by the Council for Nature was the setting up of the Conservation Corps from which has grown the **British Trust for Conservation Volunteers** (BTCV), an independent charity since 1970. The BTCV organizes volunteers to carry out conservation tasks, both in remote and beautiful country-side but increasingly in the inner city and urban fringe areas. Many traditional countryside management techniques such as coppicing, hedge laying and dry stone walling are used by conservation volunteers in work on nature reserves, in country parks and on private land and a series of very useful handbooks covering these crafts have been published.

The change in climate of opinion about wildlife and its conservation would not have taken place without the fortunate development of television. Animals and plants make compulsive viewing particularly now that colour has come to the screen.

Natural history programmes are watched by millions, whether they are the work of the BBC's long established Natural History Unit or one of the independent companies, among which Anglia's *Survival* programmes are the best known. The supply of subjects seems inexhaustible and, although the whole world is an available source, a programme about the most familiar creatures is just as popular as one on more exotic wildlife. Although television commands the largest audience, radio programmes, books and magazine articles all play an important part. The skill of the still photographer continues to improve, but not at the expense of the wildlife artist, who has now become much more than a clever illustrator.

Another and quite essential backing to the natural history and wildlife conservation movement is that provided since 1961 by the **World Wildlife Fund UK**. In 1976 £170,000 was spent on specific British projects, often to help buy a vital area for a Nature Conservation Trust or to support some essential conservation research; an almost equal amount went overseas, to save even more critical situations. In 1978 WWF-UK paid £140,020 in grants and loans for conservation in the UK. The scientific adviser of the World Wildlife Fund is the **International Union for the Conservation of Nature and Natural Resources** (IUCN) set up in 1949 to deal with the environment and all animals except birds, already covered by the **International Council for Bird Protection** (ICBP). Britain is a keen supporter of both organizations. Just as our early explorer naturalists, headed by Darwin, were concerned with the natural environment as a whole, so it is fitting that we should continue to concern ourselves with it as well as with the fate of flowers on the roadside verge and of the organisms in our village ponds. Recently more attention has been given to the wealth of opportunity that exists in cities for the conservation of their wildlife.

We have come a long way from William Turner and have seen the change of emphasis from individual naturalists to organizations with long names. But contact remains: those who have responsibility for the great campaign on behalf of our natural environment and its inhabitants like nothing better than to spend their leisure with field glasses, camera or the new gadgetry of research, enjoying what is left of the relatively untroubled world of John Ray and Gilbert White.

**Further reading**

Alexander, H. G. 1974. *Seventy years of Birdwatching.*
Berkhamsted: Poyser.

Allen, D. E. 1976. *The Naturalist in Britain: a social history.*
London: Allen Lane.

Guggisberg, C. A. W. 1977. *Early wildlife photographers.* Newton
Abbot: David and Charles.

Knowles, S. 1969. *Chorus: An anthology of bird poems.* London:
Heinemann.

Laurie, I. C. (ed.) 1979. *Nature in cities.* Chichester: Wiley.

Nicholson, E. M. 1972. *The environmental revolution.*
Harmondsworth, Middlesex: Penguin.

Park, C. C. 1976. *History of the conservation movement in Britain.*
Reading: The Conservation Trust.

Phelps, G. 1976. *Squire Waterton.* Wakefield: EP Publishing.

Ratcliffe, D. A. (ed.) 1977. *A nature conservation review.* Cambridge:
Cambridge University Press.

Raven, C. E. 1942. *John Ray, naturalist, his life and works.*
Cambridge: Cambridge University Press.

Raven, C. E. 1947. *English naturalists from Neckam to Ray: a study
of the making of the modern world.* Cambridge: Cambridge
University Press.

Sharrock, J. T. R. (ed.) 1976. *Atlas of breeding birds in Britain and
Ireland.* Tring: British Trust for Ornithology.

Sheail, J. 1976. *Nature in trust: The history of nature conservation in
Britain.* Glasgow: Blackie.

Spearman, D. 1966. *The animal anthology.* London: John Baker.

Stamp, L. D. 1969. *Nature conservation in Britain.* London: Collins.

Tansley, A. G. 1939. *The British Isles and their vegetation.*
Cambridge: Cambridge University Press.

Teagle, W. G. 1978. *The endless village.* Attingham Park: Nature
Conservancy Council.

Warren, A. & Goldsmith, F. (ed.) 1974. *Conservation in practice.*
Chichester: Wiley.

White, G. 1977. *The natural history of Selborne.* (ed. Mabey, R.)
Harmondsworth: Penguin.

# 2. Review of British habitats

Mark R. D. Seaward

Most amateur naturalists begin their studies of natural history by collecting either specimens or records of a particular group of plants or animals that happen to interest them especially. They soon find, however, that to make progress in understanding their speciality they need to extend their studies by including the subject of ecology as well. Others are attracted directly to the study of ecology in the first place.

The word ecology has had a great vogue in recent years; its meaning has been so extended and different groups of people lay emphasis on such widely differing aspects, that it is useful to give a further definition of it here. From the naturalist's point of view, ecology may be defined as the study of the relationship of plants and animals to one another and to their environment. Consequently, the study of any group of plants and animals comes to involve the consideration of other groups, and indeed it is necessary to bring in disciplines previously thought to be outside the biological field.

Naturalists interested in plants find they need to know about the weather and the soil, and so they seek information about meteorology and pedology, and ultimately about climatology and geology. Those interested in animals need to learn something of the plant communities in which the animals live, and those who start from a general consideration of the environment inevitably become involved in at least an elementary study of the taxonomy of plants and animals.

Ecologists and naturalists set out to study how organisms are distributed in, and adapted to, their environments, hoping to discover why certain animals and plants live where they do. The basis of these studies is careful observation; but it also involves measurement and experiment—and so the techniques of the mathematician, the chemist and the physicist are called upon. The interdisciplinary approach of ecology can be illustrated, for example, by reference to the study of heathlands (ill. 4).

Most modern taxonomic works (see Chapter 11) contain at least some ecological information, although the facts are usually stated very concisely. The more general works in the '*New naturalist*' series

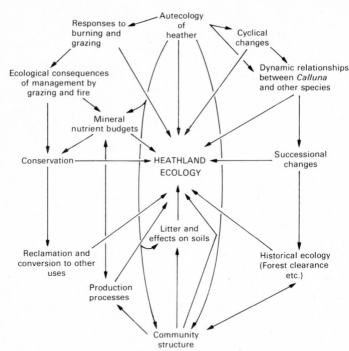

4. Main avenues of approach to heathland ecology, illustrating interactions between the various aspects of the subject (adapted from Gimingham, 1972)

published by Collins include a number of useful titles. There are also several books dealing specifically with ecology and relating particularly to Britain, including Ashby (1969), Dowdeswell (1966), McLean & Ivimey-Cook (1968) and Willis (1973). The modern quantitative approach, considering the dynamics of plant and animal communities and the energy flow through ecosystems, is covered in Lewis & Taylor (1967), Odum (1971) and Phillipson (1966); other general aspects of ecology are covered in Elton (1977) and Sankey (1964).

There are several periodicals of interest to the amateur naturalist. The *Journal of ecology*, the *Journal of animal ecology* and the

*Journal of applied ecology* are unfortunately often difficult reading because of the specialized terminology employed and the largely mathematical content of many papers; but these journals should be looked at, for they contain much useful information, even if it is sometimes difficult to disentangle. In particular, the *Biological flora of the British Isles*, which appears irregularly in the *Journal of ecology*, contains useful summaries of ecological data. For information on a local basis, the journals of the larger and more active local natural history societies and nature conservation trusts, and also the publications *Field studies* and *Biological conservation*, are useful resources.

In the field of animal ecology, there are three standard general works—Elton (1966a, 1966b) and Southwood (1977)—and several classic monographs on particular species, such as Lack (1965), Neal (1969) and Vesey-Fitzgerald (1976). Since all animals depend directly or indirectly upon plants for food, and many depend directly upon them for shelter, understanding of animal as well as plant ecology depends on a knowledge of the vegetation. Here the standard work is that of Tansley (1939).

Although in general terms the delimitation of plant communities is reasonably clear, there is still much discussion and disagreement about the classification of them. In spite of its numerical element, the classification of plant communities is still in the final analysis subjective. Rarely does the field naturalist happen upon the ideal community as described in the various publications on this subject. The best guide to this maze so far produced is Shimwell (1972). Other recommended books on British plant ecology are Tansley (1968) and Turrill (1948).

Simple classifications of vegetation based on the vertical stratification of plants, taking into consideration the animals directly or indirectly dependent upon them, can be used. These distinctive layers can be delimited above and below ground level, and above and below water level. For example, most mature woodlands are composed of the four above-ground strata: carpet layer (mainly bryophytes—mosses and liverworts), herb (or field) layer, low canopy (or shrub layer) and high canopy (see ill. 5) and, below ground, particular plant and animal populations are found at optimal depths. Similarly ponds may support plants with submerged

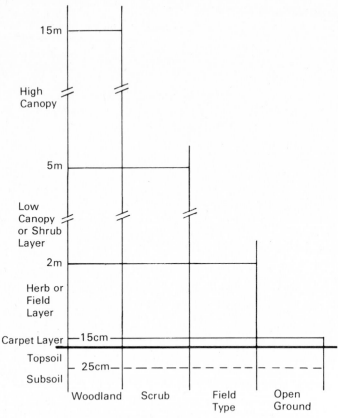

5. Plant community classification based on vertical stratification and horizontal zonation (not to scale)

leaves, floating or aerial leaves, or a combination of two or more of these characters.

Horizontal zonations can often be detected, for instance, at the margin between a woodland and grassland, and these too can be used as a basis for the classification of both plant and animal

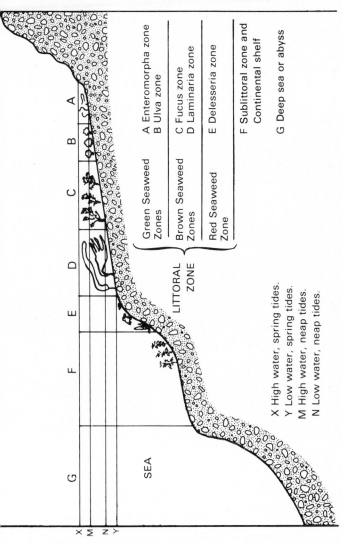

A Enteromorpha zone
B Ulva zone
C Fucus zone
D Laminaria zone
E Delesseria zone
F Sublittoral zone and Continental shelf
G Deep sea or abyss

Green Seaweed Zones
Brown Seaweed Zones
Red Seaweed Zone

LITTORAL ZONE

X High water, spring tides.
Y Low water, spring tides.
M High water, neap tides.
N Low water, neap tides.

SEA

6. Scheme to show marine zones from the shore to the open sea (not to scale) (adapted from Eales, 1967)

communities. Rocky shores (see ill. 6), gently dipping tidal mud-flats and dune systems have particularly well-defined zonations for plants and animals.

The natural progression through which a mature woodland (which is a climax community) has developed is an example of a succession or sere. The different vertical strata described above may represent different stages in the sere. When successions develop in dry and in wet conditions they are known as xeroseres and hydroseres respectively (ill. 7). In the former case, for example, bare sandy soils may develop as follows: lichens and mosses→heather→ birch→oak. In aquatic systems, the horizontal zonation, as well as the vertical stratification, will often reflect the transitional stages within the hydrosere: for example, as the level of water in a pond falls so the plants with submerged leaves will give way to those with floating leaves and eventually they may be replaced by a reed swamp, and if alkaline conditions predominate, alder and willow will become established, followed by ash or even beech woodland as

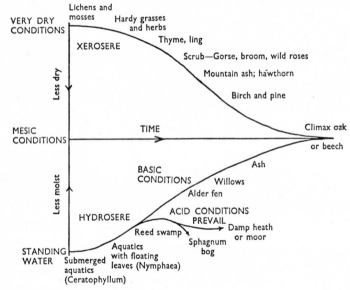

7. Major successions (seres) in the British Isles (from Ashby, 1969)

the drying out process continues.

   The following classification of major habitats to be found in the British Isles is by no means definitive, and a wide variety of schemes may be adopted (e.g. habitat recording cards of the Biological Records Centre, see p. 82, and the Nature Conservation Trusts). In this chapter the three broadly-defined ecosystems—aquatic, terrestrial and artificial—have been used as a basis, but it is naturally difficult to maintain a rigid system of classification when mixed habitats (ecotones), such as bogs and marshes with both aquatic and terrestrial characteristics, are a common feature of the British landscape.

## Aquatic

### Marine/Maritime
The distribution of plants is mainly related to light penetration: the larger algae occur in intertidal and subtidal regions, and the microscopic algae, constituting the phytoplankton, occur in the

| Name of site : | | | | | | | | | Parish : | | |
|---|---|---|---|---|---|---|---|---|---|---|---|
| Acreage : | | Grid Ref. | | | | | | Access : | Private | Roadside | Right of Way |
| Name and address of Owner/Tenant *(if known)* | | | | | | | | | | | |
| Type of pit | Sand | | Gravel | | Chalk | | Limestone | | Clay | | |
| Uses | Working | | Abandoned | | Fishing | | Water sport | | Picnics | | Game rearing |
| Condition | Clean | | Litter | | Slight tipping | | Heavy tipping | | | | |
| Habitats | Deep water | | Shallow water | | Floating plants | | Reedbeds | | Marsh | | Bare ground |
| | Grassland | | Heath | | Tall herb | | Scrub | | Woodland | | Cliff |
| Indicators | Orchids | | Marjoram | | Eyebright | | Harebells | | Heather | | Birch |
| | Badger set | | Warblers nesting | | Blue butterflies | | Brown butterflies | | Sand Martins | | Lizards |
| | Reedmace | | Sedges | | Dragonflies | | Ducks | | Coots | | Grebes |
| | Frogs | | Toads | | Newts | | Pike | | Minnow | | Tench |
| Name of Surveyor | ................................................................................ | | | | | | | | Date : | | |
| Address | ................................................................................ | | | | | | | | | | |

8. Example of a habitat recording card: survey of ponds, pits and quarries by the Lincolnshire Trust for Nature Conservation

upper layers of the open sea where light penetrates. Associated with the great diversity and abundance of phytoplankton in the sunlit layers are the planktonic animals (zooplankton), in similar diversity and abundance, which include the young and adult stages of small crustaceans and the young of lobsters, crabs, barnacles and fishes. These feed on plants and their numbers are therefore closely related to phytoplankton numbers. An excellent introduction to plankton is given in Hardy (1971).

Other factors, such as wave action and the nature of the substrate are also important in influencing plant and animal distribution in marine habitats. A wide range of habitats from sandy and silty shores to pebble beaches of shingle or boulders to rocks and cliffs are to be found around the British Isles. The flowering plants of many of these habitats are admirably covered in Hepburn (1952). These areas are also important for geological study.

For introductory and general accounts of sea-shore life, the following are recommended: Barrett & Yonge (1958), Campbell (1976), Ford (1964), Haas & Knorr (1966), Prud'homme van Reine (1962) and Yonge (1966). A more specialized account of animal ecology is provided by Eales (1967), and detailed information on algal and lichen ecology of rocky shores is given in Lewis (1976) and Fletcher (1973a, 1973b) respectively.

Zonation is readily observed on rocky shores, though in detail it is greatly affected by exposure and other local factors. A useful referent when comparing the zonation of different rocky shores is the barnacle line, which remains constant in relation to average tide levels.

The bird life of these areas is particularly worthy of investigation; there are many books on general bird identification, behaviour, etc., but the works by Cramp et al. (1974), Gibson-Hill (1976) and Tuck & Heinzel (1978) specifically cater for the marine ornithologist.

*Estuarine*
The mixing of salt and fresh water, as for example at a river mouth, provides an interesting ecological setting: the plants and animals found here have wide tolerances and cope with the continual fluctuation in water salinity. The type of estuarine community depends mainly upon the physiography of the coastline. Extensive,

almost level mud deposits, known as flats, may be devoid of
vascular plants. Areas colonized, and to a large extent stabilized, by
vascular plants are known as salt marshes; they bear highly
distinctive plant zonation (ill. 9). Coastal lagoons and swamps,
which often develop in sand-dune complexes, and pools and lakes,
which are influenced directly by sea spray and/or occasional high
tides, usually support similar plant and animal communities.

9. Salt marsh community, Shingle Street, Suffolk, showing characteristic plant zonation
(photo: P. J. Shaw)

Relatively few animal species are native in estuarine habitats, such are the variations in salinity, temperature and water movement. Good introductions are provided by Angel (1975), Barnes (1974, 1979), McLuskey (1971) and many specialized papers dealing with these habitats are to be found in a variety of journals, but general or comprehensive works, such as Boorman and Ranwell (1977), Chapman (1960), Eltringham (1971) and Ranwell (1972), are few in number.

## Freshwater

Classification of freshwater habitats depends upon water movement and/or mineral content. Standing water (lentic) habitats, such as pools, ponds and lakes, are classified according to size and/or depth of water, varying from puddles, pools, ponds (less than 1 ha or 2.5 acres), medium lakes (1 to 40 ha or 2.5 to 100 acres) to large lakes (more than 40 ha or 100 acres). Such habitats may have a significant inflow and outflow, but water movement is often promoted by wind action only.

Shallow ponds and lakes naturally contain considerable rooted vegetation, whereas deeper waters support aquatic plants only at their margins, because insufficient light penetrates for plant growth. The algal ecology of most standing water habitats is particularly worthy of investigation, as are the zooplankton and the vertebrate feeders (fish, amphibians and birds).

Running water (lotic) habitats are usually classified according to speed of flow, which is proportional to oxygen concentration. Some species of plants and animals are found in both standing and running water, whereas others are characteristic of one habitat only; for example, stonefly nymphs are found only in the upper fast-flowing reaches of streams and rivers free from pollution.

The piping of domestic and industrial effluents into some streams, rivers and lakes may result in extremely low availability of oxygen. Many plants and animals are particularly good indicators of such polluted conditions (see Hynes 1963).

Standing or running waters poor in nutrients are described as oligotrophic, and those rich in nutrients are described as eutrophic. In upland areas of the north and west of the British Isles, oligo-trophic waters are often fed almost entirely from chemicals supplied in rainfall. In agricultural areas surface and underground water often receives an excess of chemicals, such as nitrogen and phosphorus, which are derived from the application of fertilizers to the land; this condition (eutrophication) is usually to the detriment of most organisms—only a few species flourish in such conditions, and these may be used as indicators of over-enrichment.

Mires, subdivided into bogs (acidic) and fens (alkaline) are often included in terrestrial ecosystem classification; they vary according to their topographical setting (e.g. upland, flood plain, basin, valley) and their nutrient status.

The following books, together with the publications of the Freshwater Biological Association (see p. 148), cover most aspects of freshwater ecology: Clegg (1974), Hynes (1970), Macan (1959, 1974), Macan & Worthington (1974), Mellanby (1975), Prud'homme van Reine (1957) and Ward & Whipple (1969); a detailed bibliography is provided by Mortimer (1976).

## Terrestrial

### Woodland

Deciduous and coniferous woodlands are common over large areas of the British Isles, but in many parts of England mature woodlands, and indeed trees, are fast disappearing. Nevertheless, a wide range of woodland types is still to be found, which may be classified as follows: birch/oak, ash, beech, alder, mixed deciduous (various combinations of elm, ash, oak, hornbeam, lime, sweet chestnut, willow, hazel, etc.) and pine (ill. 10).

The presence or absence of a shrub layer (less than 5 m or 15 feet high; (see ill. 5) is an important characteristic of woodlands; for instance, oak, birch and pine woods in upland areas are usually devoid of this layer, as are pure beechwoods in south-east England. Shrub layers in the British Isles vary according to the influence of the dominant trees, climate, soil type and woodland management (ill. 11); hazel, hawthorn, holly, elder, wild roses and brambles are particularly common in this role, as is the introduced rhododendron, which has become a hindrance to good forestry management.

Coniferous plantations, mainly of larch and Sitka spruce, are a common, indeed often a dominant, feature of the British landscape today (ill. 12). Planted woodlands and parklands around large houses are also a rich source of mature trees, in particular sycamore, horse chestnut, beech, lime, and a wide variety of introduced deciduous and coniferous species.

Hedgerows (see Pollard *et al.*, 1974) also provide the setting for large numbers of mature trees, but sadly these are disappearing due

10. Scots pine (*Pinus sylvestris*) at Glen Affric: a remnant of the old Caledonian forest (photo: P. J. Shaw)

to changes in agricultural practices; more recently the spread of Dutch elm disease is eliminating one of the characteristic hedgerow trees. The once-rich epiphytic flora associated with mature trees has also disappeared over much of England due mainly to air pollution; the epiphytic lichen communities that remain, mainly in the north and west of the British Isles, are described in detail in Seaward (1977).

11. A form of woodland management: coppicing in Hayley Wood, Cambridgeshire (photo: P. J. Shaw)

12.  Small plantation of Scots pine (*Pinus sylvestris*) showing the influence of prevailing wind on the overall shape (photo: M. R. D. Seaward)

13.  Linwood Warren, a lowland heath in north Lincolnshire, showing birch invasion into the heather-dominated area (foreground) in which the locally-rare lichen Iceland Moss (*Cetraria islandica*) is to be found (photo: M. R. D. Seaward)

Immature woodland (mainly birch) and scrublands, composed of hazel, hawthorn, blackthorn, box, juniper or various other rarer species, are widespread; these may either develop naturally through succession or be caused by land mismanagement over a variety of heathlands, grasslands, etc. in lowland areas.

A wide range of woodland ecology topics is to be found in Darlington (1966), Ford (1959), Neal (1958), Ovington (1965), Simms (1971) and Southwood (1965); these books provide useful information on the variety of animal life to be found in woodlands, particularly insects, many of which are pests of trees. The role of trees in the British landscape is well described in Edlin (1974) and Rackham (1976). Many guides to British trees have been published in recent years, and a few of the more useful of these are listed in Chapter 11; the many useful publications of the Forestry Commission (see p. 163) should also be consulted.

## Heaths and grasslands

The classification of these habitats is complex, but is generally based on the influence of minerals (acidic or calcareous), water regime, altitude and management (see Boatman 1979; Moore 1966).

Lowland acidic heaths and grasslands

These are frequent on soils, which are usually podsolic and infertile, in unwooded areas of lowland Britain (broadly defined as the region to the south-east of a line between the rivers Humber and Severn). They are referred to as heathlands, commons or warrens in different parts of this region (ill. 13). The drier areas are usually dominated by heather, bell heather or a variety of grasses, and in the south and west of England and Wales, by gorse. Bracken and rose bay willow herb are becoming increasingly important on dry heathland. Generally speaking, acidic heaths and grasslands have a limited diversity of vascular plant species, but this is not so for bryophytes and lichens.

The competition between the different plant species and the effects of rabbits and game birds in these communities produce significant changes, and field investigations of these interactions would repay further study. Amphibians, reptiles and a wide range of invertebrates, with the exception of molluscs, are also found, but

14. Upland moorland, Northumberland: a vegetational pattern of heather (*Calluna vulgaris*) and bracken (*Pteridium aquilinum*) (photo: P. J. Shaw)

investigations of animal communities in general have received relatively less attention than corresponding work on plants in these habitats.

A variety of acidic mires (bogs) may result from periodic or continual waterlogging; such areas may be dominated by cross-leaved bell heather and/or a variety of sedges, rushes or grasses.

Upland acidic heaths and grasslands
These are more usually referred to as moorlands (ill. 14), and are mainly distributed in relatively high rainfall areas in the north and west of the British Isles. The flora is similar to that of lowland heaths and grasslands, but a wide variety of regional differences exist. Summit communities, on shallow soils amongst frost-shattered rock debris, are affected by exposure and the grazing habits of deer, sheep, feral goats, hares, game birds, etc. The vegetation here is

composed of cushion-forming mosses, lichens and scattered herbs and grasses. Waterlogged areas on plateaux and lower slopes support sedges, rushes, mat grass, purple moor grass, cotton grass, bryophytes, and a limited number of herb species. As well as the many articles on lowland and upland heaths and grasslands which have appeared in the *Journal of Ecology*, the following books are recommended: Darling (1978), Friedlander (1960), Gimingham (1972, 1975), McVean & Ratcliffe (1962), Pearsall (1972) and Tansley (1939).

Calcareous grasslands

These are to be found on a variety of geological formations. In general the major calcareous rock formations are geographically separated in the British Isles, with chalk in the south and east, and limestone in the north and west. Calcareous grassland floras are both varied and rich in species: they vary according to the influences of soils, which usually range from neutral (pH, 6.5) to strongly alkaline (pH, 8.5), climate, altitude and/or management. These variations include habitats such as (a) limestone pavements which support a rich fern and bryophyte flora in their fissures (grykes) and a diverse lichen flora on their flat horizontal surfaces (clints)— mature woodlands in such areas are rare in Britain (ill. 15), (b) screes and cliffs with shallow soil pockets, (c) grasslands and meadows with a high organic matter, and (d) soils with various levels of drainage impedance giving rise to flushes, marshes and alkaline mires (fens).

Calcareous grassland also develops in some of the volcanic rock areas of southern England, on shelly sand areas around the coast. For further information on various aspects of calcareous grassland ecology consult the many articles relating to the Malham area which have appeared in *Field Studies* and the books by Godwin (1978), Lousley (1969) and Sankey (1966).

*Natural habitats low in organic content*

These include such habitats as dunes, rock debris (see p. 50) and outcrops; they are often dominated by bryophytes and lichens, which provide food and shelter for a variety of invertebrates (see Duffey, 1968). Many cryptogamic (flowerless) plants are particularly

15. Colt Park Wood National Nature Reserve: a fine example of mature woodland on limestone pavement (photo: P. J. Shaw)

good environmental indicators, having specific pH and/or mineral requirements.

The importance of these plants in the colonization of, and the succession on, bare soil and rock surfaces is covered in numerous articles to be found in the *Journal of Bryology* (formerly *Transactions of the British Bryological Society*) and *The Lichenologist*, and their role in community structure is given in McVean & Ratcliffe (1962), Seaward (1977) and Tansley (1939).

## Artificial

### Agricultural

Perhaps the most important influences on plant and animal ecology today are brought about by the activities of man. These anthropogenic factors have been highly significant over the past 6,000 years since the development of agriculture, which necessitated the destruction of natural habitats by felling, burning, ploughing, grazing, lowering the water table, etc., with the loss of large tracts of forest. Associated with these practices has been the spread of plants (ill. 16) and animals, often introduced species, which favour habitats created or influenced by man; such organisms are referred to as being synanthropic.

16. Rosebay willow-herb (*Chamaenerion angustifolium*): an aggressive 'weed' of disturbed ground, shown here dominating a woodland clearing (photo: M. R. D. Seaward)

More intensive agricultural practices, mainly following the enclosure of land in the eighteenth century, have resulted in the rise of 'monoagriculture', whereby a few species dominate very large areas of the countryside either directly as crops or indirectly as grazing animals. More recently, the extensive use of agricultural chemicals and the removal of hedgerows have been detrimental to both fauna and flora.

Nevertheless, agricultural habitats are worthy of investigation by the naturalist, although few ecological guides are available on the subject, exceptions being Cheatle (1976), Hawksworth (1974), Pollard et al. (1974) and Salisbury (1964).

*Urban and industrial*
The increased rate of development of the 'urban ecosystem' of brick, concrete and tarmacadam, and the pollution of air, water and soil, have been major factors in the dramatic environmental changes in Britain over the past two centuries. A very wide range of artificial habitats has been created in urban areas, including gardens, shrubberies, parks and roadside trees, recreational land including golf courses, churchyards and cemeteries, waste land, disused railway tracks and cuttings, quays and docks, refuse tips, sewage farms and reservoirs, and walls and buildings made of a variety of materials, which support a wealth of plant and animal life.

Inter-urban man-made habitats of interest to the naturalist include green lanes, hedgerows, walls and road verges including motorway banks, railway cuttings, bridges, disused airfields, canals, drainage ditches and reservoirs.

Artificial habitats created by industry are to be found in both urban and rural settings; these include mines, spoil heaps, quarries (ill. 17), gravel pits and derelict buildings.

Unfortunately many of these habitats are associated with various kinds of pollution which are detrimental to all but a few organisms. Nevertheless, man-made habitats provide the naturalist with ample scope for fieldwork although only a few ecological books are available on the subject, e.g. Chinery (1977), Darlington (1969), Fitter (1945), Goodman et al. (1965), Hawksworth & Rose (1976), Hynes (1963), Mabey (1978), Owen (1978), Salisbury (1964) and Simms (1975).

17. Plant colonization of an abandoned chalk quarry at Wharram, now a nature reserve belonging to the Yorkshire Trust for Nature Conservation (photo: P. J. Shaw)

Soil, although omitted directly from the above analysis, can also be regarded as an ecosystem: besides forming the medium for terrestrial plant growth, it supports a very extensive fauna and flora. The latter consists of vast numbers of bacteria, fungi and algae, together with the dormant stages of higher plants. A wide range of animal life, from nematodes, annelids and insects to burrowing vertebrates, is to be found in soils; invertebrates are particularly abundant where the soil organic content is high.

For a general account of soil see Russell (1961), and for a more detailed account of the animal component see Kevan (1962) and Kühnelt (1976). Jackson & Raw (1966) suggest a number of investigations on soil animals.

This review of British habitats is by no means exhaustive; furthermore, it gives only a limited indication of the interdisciplinary

18. Soil erosion beneath beech (*Fagus sylvatica*) woodland, the result of recreation pressure – unmanaged (photo: M. R. D. Seaward)

nature of the subject. Regional and local studies, ranging from major vegetational surveys (e.g. Burnett 1964; McVean & Ratcliffe 1962) to detailed ecological investigations of relatively small woodlands (e.g. Rackham 1975; Steele & Welch 1973), provide the naturalist with both reference material and a foundation on which to base an individual or group project.

Similar regional source material can be found in the *Handbooks* which are published annually by the British Association for the Advancement of Science as guides to the areas around the different conference centres, in the *Atlases* of the British fauna and flora (see Chapter 4, p. 85), in *Floras* which are available for most counties, in Collins' '*New Naturalist*' series (e.g. Condry 1966; Edwards *et al.* 1962; Ellis 1965), and in journals of local natural history societies and nature conservation trusts. The recent works on *Upper Teesdale* (Clapham 1978) and on *Fenland* (Godwin 1978) exemplify to good effect the ecological approach to a regional study.

Other overviews of British ecological studies should consider past and present climate (e.g. Manley 1952), associated flora (see Pennington 1974; Godwin 1975; Perring & Walters 1976; Perring &

Sell 1968), and major landscape changes (e.g. Hoskins 1970; Stamp 1969; Rackham 1976).

   Consideration should also be given to determining detrimental effects brought about by man's activities on the fauna and flora (e.g. Arvill 1976; Carson 1965; Christian 1966; Mellanby 1970), to evaluating sites (ill. 18) and species worthy of conservation (see Ratcliffe 1977) and to taking steps to preserve them (see Stamp 1970; Usher 1973; also Chapters 4 and 9).

## References

Angel, H. 1975. *The world of an estuary*. London: Faber.

Arvill, R. 1976. *Man and environment*. Harmondsworth: Penguin.

Ashby, M. 1969. *Introduction to plant ecology*. London: Macmillan.

Barnes, R. S. K. 1974. *Estuarine biology*. London: Arnold.

Barnes, R. S. K. 1979. *Coasts and estuaries*. London: Hodder & Stoughton.

Barrett, J. H. & Yonge, C. M. 1958. *Collins pocket guide to the sea shore*. London: Collins.

Boatman, D. J. 1979. *Fields and lowlands*. London: Hodder & Stoughton.

Boorman, L. A. & Ranwell, D. S. 1977. *Ecology of Maplin Sands and the coastal zones of Suffolk, Essex and North Kent*. Cambridge: Institute of Terrestrial Ecology.

Burnett, J. H. (ed.) 1964. *The vegetation of Scotland*. Edinburgh: Oliver & Boyd.

Campbell, A. C. 1976. *The Hamlyn guide to the seashore and shallow seas of Britain and Europe*. London: Hamlyn.

Carson, R. 1965. *Silent spring*. Harmondsworth: Penguin.

Chapman, V. J. 1960. *Salt marshes and salt deserts of the world*. London: Leonard Hill.

Cheatle, J. R. W. 1976. *A guide to the British landscape*. London: Collins.

Chinery, M. 1977. *The natural history of the garden*. London: Collins.

Christian, G. 1966. *Tomorrow's countryside*. London: Murray.

Clapham, A. R. (ed.) 1978. *Upper Teesdale. The area and its natural history*. London: Collins.

Clegg, J. 1974. *Freshwater life*. London: Warne.

Condry, W. M. 1966. *The Snowdonia National Park*. London: Collins.

Cramp, S., Bourne, W. R. P. & Saunders, D. 1974. *The seabirds of Britain and Ireland*. London: Collins.

Darlington, A. (ed.) 1966. *Woodland life in colour*. London: Blandford.

Darlington, A. 1966. *Ecology of refuse tips*. London: Heinemann.

Darlington, A. (ed.) 1978. *Mountains and moorlands*. London: Hodder & Stoughton.

Dowdeswell, W. H. 1966. *An introduction to animal ecology*. London: Methuen.

Duffey, E. 1968. An ecological analysis of the spider fauna of sand dunes. *Journal of Animal Ecology*, **37**, 641–74.

Eales, N. B. 1967. *The littoral fauna of Great Britain*, 4th edn. Cambridge: Cambridge University Press.

Edlin, H. L. 1974. *Trees, woods and man*. London: Collins.

Edwards, K. C., Swinnerton, H. H. & Hall, T. H. 1962. *The Peak District*. London: Collins.

Ellis, E. A. (ed.) 1965. *The Broads*. London: Collins.

Elton, C. S. 1966*a*. *Animal ecology*. London: Methuen.

Elton, C. S. 1966*b*. *The pattern of animal communities*. London: Methuen.

Elton, C. S. 1977. *The ecology of invasions by animals and plants*. London: Methuen.

Eltringham, S. K. 1971. *Life in mud and sand*. London: English Universities Press.

Fitter, R. S. R. 1945. *London's natural history*. London: Collins.

Fletcher, A. 1973*a*. The ecology of marine (littoral) lichens on some rocky shores of Anglesey. *Lichenologist*, **5**, 368–400.

Fletcher, A. 1973*b*. The ecology of maritime (supralittoral) lichens on some rocky shores of Anglesey. *Lichenologist*, **5**, 401–22.

Ford, V. E. 1959. *How to begin your field work: woodland*. London: Murray.

Ford, V. E. 1964. *How to begin your field work: the seashore*. London: Murray.

Friedlander, C. P. 1960. *Heathland ecology*. London: Heinemann.

Gibson-Hill, C. A. 1976. *A guide to the birds of the coast*. (rev. by B. Campbell, R. Campbell & R. Prytherch). London: Constable.

Gimingham, C. H. 1972. *Ecology of heathlands*. London: Chapman & Hall.

Gimingham, C. H. 1975. *An introduction to heathland ecology*. Edinburgh: Oliver & Boyd.

Godwin, H. 1975. *The history of the British flora*. London: Cambridge University Press.

Godwin, H. 1978. *Fenland: its ancient past and uncertain future*. Cambridge: Cambridge University Press.

Goodman, G. T., Edwards, R. W. & Lambert, J. M. (ed.) 1965. *Ecology and the industrial society*. Oxford: Blackwell.

Haas, W. de & Knorr, F. 1966. *The young specialist looks at marine life*. London: Burke.

Hardy, A. C. 1971. *The open sea: the world of plankton*. London: Collins.

Hawksworth, D. L. (ed.) 1974. *The changing flora and fauna of Britain*. London: Academic Press.

Hawksworth, D. L. & Rose, F. 1976. *Lichens as pollution monitors*. London: Arnold.

Hepburn, I. 1952. *Flowers of the Coast*. London: Collins.

Hoskins, W. G. 1970. *The making of the English landscape*. Harmondsworth: Penguin.

Hynes, H. B. N. 1963. *The biology of polluted waters*. Liverpool: Liverpool University Press.

Hynes, H. B. N. 1970. *The ecology of running waters*. Liverpool: Liverpool University Press.

Jackson, R. M. & Raw, F. 1966. *Life in the soil*. London: Arnold.

Kevan, D. K. McE. 1962. *Soil animals: aspects of zoology*. London: Witherby.

Kühnelt, W. 1976. *Soil biology*. London: Faber.

Lack, D. 1965. *The life of a robin*. London: Witherby.

Lewis, J. R. 1976. *The ecology of rocky shores*. London: Hodder & Stoughton.

Lewis, T. & Taylor, L. R. 1967. *Introduction to experimental ecology*. London: Academic Press.

Lousley, J. E. 1969. *Wild flowers of chalk and limestone*. London: Collins.

Mabey, R. 1978. *The unofficial countryside*. London: Sphere.

Macan, T. T. 1959. *A guide to freshwater invertebrate animals*. London: Longman.

Macan, T. T. 1974. *Freshwater ecology*. London: Longman.

Macan, T. T. & Worthington, E. B. 1974. *Life in lakes and rivers*. London: Collins.

McLean, R. C. & Ivimey-Cook, W. R. 1968. *Practical field ecology*. London: Allen & Unwin.

McLusky, D. S. 1971. *Ecology of estuaries*. London: Heinemann.

McVean, D. N. & Ratcliffe, D. A. 1962. *Plant communities of the Scottish Highlands*. London: HMSO.

Manley, G. 1952. *Climate and the British scene*. London: Collins.

Mellanby, H. 1975. *Animal life in freshwater. A guide to British freshwater invertebrates*. London: Chapman & Hall.

Mellanby, K. 1970. *Pesticides and pollution*. London: Collins.

Moore, I. 1966. *Grass and grasslands*. London: Collins.

Mortimer, M. A. E. 1976. Looking at life in freshwater. *Natural History Book Reviews*, **1**, 58–65.

Neal, E. 1958. *Woodland ecology*. London: Heinemann.

Neal, E. 1969. *The badger*. London: Collins.

Odum, E. P. 1971. *Fundamentals of ecology*. Eastbourne: Holt-Saunders.

Ovington, J. D. 1965. *Woodlands*. London: English Universities Press.

Owen, D. 1978. *Towns and gardens*. London: Hodder & Stoughton.

Pearsall, W. H. 1972. *Mountains and moorlands*. (rev. by W. Pennington). London: Collins.

Pennington, W. 1974. *The history of British vegetation*. London: English Universities Press.

Perring, F. H. & Sell, P. D. (eds.) 1968. *Critical supplement to the Atlas of the British Flora*. London: Nelson.

Perring, F. H. & Walters, S. M. (eds.) 1976. *Atlas of the British Flora*. Wakefield: EP Publishing.

Phillipson, J. 1966. *Ecological energetics*. London: Arnold.

Pollard, E., Hooper, M. D. & Moore, N. W. 1974. *Hedges*. London: Collins.

Prud'homme van Reine, W. J. 1957. *Plants and animals of pond and stream*. London: Murray.

Prud'homme van Reine, W. J. 1962. *Plants and animals of the seashore*. London: Murray.

Rackham, O. 1975. *Hayley Wood. Its history and ecology*. Cambridge: Cambridgeshire and Isle of Ely Naturalists' Trust.

Rackham, O. 1976. *Trees and woodlands in the British landscape*. London: Dent.

Ranwell, D. S. 1972. *Ecology of salt marshes and sand dunes*. London: Chapman & Hall.

Ratcliffe, D. A. (ed.) 1977. *A nature conservation review*. Cambridge: Cambridge University Press.

Russell, E. J. 1961. *The world of the soil*. London: Collins.

Salisbury, E. J. 1964. *Weeds and aliens*. London: Collins.

Sankey, J. 1964. *A guide to field biology*. London: Longman.

Sankey, J. 1966. *Chalkland ecology*. London: Heinemann.

Seaward, M. R. D. (ed.) 1977. *Lichen ecology*. London: Academic Press.

Shimwell, D. W. 1972. *Description and classification of vegetation*. London: Sidgwick and Jackson.

Simms, E. 1971. *Woodland birds*. London: Collins.

Simms, E. 1975. *Birds of town and suburb*. London: Collins.

Southwood, T. R. E. 1963. *Life of the wayside and woodland*. London: Warne.

Southwood, T. R. E. 1971. *Ecological methods*. London: Chapman & Hall.

Stamp, L. D. 1969. *Man and the land*. London: Collins.

Stamp, L. D. 1970. *Nature conservation in Britain*. London: Collins.

Steele, R. C. & Welch, R. C. (eds.) 1973. *Monks Wood. A nature reserve record*. Monks Wood: Nature Conservancy.

Tansley, A. G. 1939. *The British Isles and their vegetation*. Cambridge: Cambridge University Press.

Tansley, A. G. 1968. *Britain's green mantle: past, present and future*. (rev. by M. C. F. Proctor). London: Allen & Unwin.

Tuck, G. & Heinzel, H. 1978. *Field guide to seabirds of Britain and the world*. London: Collins.

Turrill, W. B. 1948. *British plant life*. London: Collins.

Usher, M. B. 1973. *Biological management and conservation*. London: Chapman & Hall.

Vesey-Fitzgerald, B. 1976. *Town fox, country fox*. London: White Lion Press.

Ward, M. B. & Whipple, G. E. 1969. *Freshwater biology* (rev. by W. T. Edmunson). New York: Wiley.

Willis, A. J. 1973. *Introduction to plant ecology. A guide for beginners in the study of plant communities*. London: Allen & Unwin.

Yonge, C. M. 1966. *The sea shore*. London: Collins.

# 3. Fieldwork and equipment

Martin Spray and Peter J. Prosser

There are two types of naturalist—the passive and the active. The first is satisfied by natural history on television, in talks and in books whereas the second prefers to gain information from personal experience in the field.

By joining a natural history society, the beginner can go out into the field with experienced naturalists, who can point out features of interest which might otherwise be missed, and provide names for the plants and animals encountered. This should not be the endpoint of involvement; one's own fieldwork is infinitely more satisfying. A naturalist ought to be able to do at least five things: *observe* accurately, *identify*, *record* and *understand* what has been observed, and *use* the records.

## Observation

Fieldwork often begins as a form of entertainment; but it should develop as a sort of casual education. The amount of pleasure that is derived from fieldwork does not, of course, depend upon the vigour with which the work is pursued; but the total benefit certainly increases with additional commitment and effort put in during fieldwork. Worthwhile results are only achieved through accurate observation. Much practice is needed before a naturalist is able to make accurate observations. For instance it is surprisingly difficult to judge size and distance; there may be twice or only half as many birds as the observer estimated in a flock; and even the most experienced fieldworkers can expect to overlook some of the most interesting things on their first visit to an area.

Only a minimum of equipment is necessary to aid observation: binoculars and a hand lens cater for the needs of all but the specialist such as the microscopist. However, endless patience and perseverence are essential, and the ability to concentrate on one object even when surrounded by other distractions is difficult to learn, but necessary.

Observation improves with practice. Try making accurate counts, detailing the behaviour of animals, estimating and then measuring sizes and distances. Do not be put off if details are missed or if inaccurate estimates are made in the first instance. Practice can easily be gained by making routine notes on familiar ground, such as every evening when walking the dog, or between bouts of gardening, or on the way to school or work. If done well, this type of routine observation can produce valuable information. Things are often overlooked because they are so familiar to the observer that he tends to ignore them.

## Identification

Sooner or later, the names of plants and animals become important. Without their names it is not easy to find out more about, or even tell other people about, what has been seen. Fortunately the wealth of plant and animal life, at least in Britain, can now be named, though some of the names are difficult to remember. To confuse the picture, for some groups (especially the flowering plants, some of the vertebrates, and many insects) English and Latin names are used almost equally.

It is impractical and not advisable to carry a large number of reference books in the field for obvious reasons, and in any case identification is often a slow process and can absorb too much time in the field. However, when beginning serious fieldwork use of an identification book will be needed until the mechanics of it have been mastered, and some of the commoner species of the group can be quickly recognized. The experienced naturalist does carry some books amongst his baggage: for example, a botanist is likely to use the *Excursion flora of the British Isles* regularly.

Recent legislation (see Chapter 9) has restricted the naturalist's freedom to take home specimens he could not identify, and as a general principle collect *nothing* unless you are convinced that it is needed. However, the dangers of collecting have sometimes been exaggerated. The removal of a snail or a beetle, a clump of moss, or a small piece of flowering plant, has a negligible impact, and may be necessary before the species can be accurately identified. In all cases, however, *be convinced that the specimen is really necessary*, and *take as little and as few as possible*. Remember too, that damage to the surroundings by trampling, etc. is often more detrimental than the loss of a specimen; therefore *disturb as little as possible*. Accepting that specimens are needed on certain occasions, do not waste them.

Label each clearly with date, location and habitat details, and place in a suitable container. Unless they are to be dealt with together, keep each specimen and its label separate. If they are live invertebrates that need to be kept moist, place a little damp vegetation or paper with them. If the specimens are damp, sort through them as soon as possible, or they may die before they can be named.

Some species may prove too difficult to identify. These may be referred to an expert for naming, but always provide a specimen that is likely to show all the features by which it can be recognised: some people *can* name a grass from a broken leaf-blade, or a beetle from a wing-case but they are exceptional.

## Recording

Much better than fully-labelled bags and boxes of specimens is a field notebook full of the names of the plants and animals that have been found (some of the names, of course, added afterwards); details of where they were seen, how common they were, and what they were doing; and perhaps quick sketches that will assist later identification, or sketch-maps that will enable them to be found again.

Many naturalists begin recording their observations in the form of a diary. This is often frowned on, for diaries have two great disadvantages: their contents are usually rather haphazard, and they tend to be too subjective to be useful later. Moreover, they are not usually written in the field. They can, however, give immense pleasure afterwards, and they encourage the habit of regular notemaking.

There is an art to making notes. The example from a naturalist's notebook shown in ill. 19 shows how careful and succinct they can be. A naturalist should never be without a pencil, or better still, pencils, especially when used on a rainy day. All notes should be dated, and the locality given, preferably with a detailed map reference. Besides the objects of interest themselves (and any specimens collected should be referred to in the notes, perhaps by a number), it is useful to note the weather conditions and time of day. Sometimes the names of companions, who may be able to confirm an observation at a later date should be noted: full details and

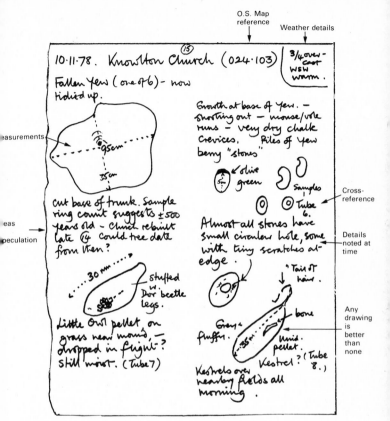

O.S. Map reference

Weather details

10·11·78. Knowlton Church (024·103) ⑬ 3/4 overcast WSW warm.

Fallen Yew (one of 6) – now tidied up.

Measurements

95cm

35cm

Growth at base of Yew. – shooting out – mouse/vole runs – very dry chalk crevices. Piles of Yew berry "stones"

olive green (5m)

Samples

Tube 6.

Almost all stones have small circular hole, some with tiny scratches at edge.

Cross-reference

Details noted at time

Cut base of trunk. Sample ring count suggests ±500 years old – Church rebuilt late C4 could tree date from then?

Areas

Speculation

30 mm

stuffed w. Dor beetle legs.

Little Owl pellet on grass near mound, – dropped in fright? Still moist. (Tube 7)

"Tail" of hair.

bone

Grey fluffy.

Unid. pellet.

Kestrel ? (Tube 8.)

Kestrels over nearby fields all morning.

Any drawing is better than none

19. Facsimile page from field-notebook – part of an animal feeding study at the site of a ruined church

verification will be necessary to persuade others that a rarity has been seen.

Very few notebooks contain all the detail they should: there always seems to be good reasons, especially on an exposed site in a biting wind, why the writing should be postponed until later. Writing up full records 'on the spot' is one of the most difficult disciplines, yet it must become a habit, if the work is to have serious value. To save time, an experienced worker develops his own shorthand, signs and abbreviations. The skill of making rapid diagrams and sketch-maps is well worth acquiring; any attempt at drawing is better than none.

It is often necessary to make a subsequent fair copy of one's fieldnotes. Notebooks can be a jumble of details, which should later be organized. Besides this, notebooks are easily lost. Some people prefer to use perforated notebooks, or spiral-bound reporter's pads, and to begin their notes on each new topic on a clean sheet. These can then be torn from the pad, and placed in appropriate files.

If a particular group of plants or animals is being studied, field notes may afterwards be transferred to record cards such as those provided by the Biological Records Centre (see Chapter 4). If such an investigation is being undertaken seriously, it may be best to use record cards in the field, as this can save considerable time; if so, a notebook for a full record of site, habitat, etc., should also be kept. Improvised record sheets can be easily produced, either on a duplicating machine or with carbon paper, for frequent similar observations on a particular species or location.

Besides notebooks and record sheets, a camera can be invaluable, particularly when faced with the problem of whether to collect a specimen for identification, or if a general picture of a site is needed. Some sort of scale object (a ruler for example) is often important, if other details in the photograph do not make the scale obvious.

For some purposes, for instance when working at night, or in wet weather, or for making very rapid notes, a small tape recorder is very useful. However, it has the grave disadvantage of requiring a considerable amount of time for subsequent transcription. Paper and pencil are nearly always more satisfactory.

All successful naturalists spend much of their time reading about their special interests, interpreting their notes, and planning future fieldwork. In fact, the more expert one becomes, the more time one is likely to spend in this way. These aspects of natural history can often be fitted in when bad weather prevents fieldwork.

This begs the question of *what* branch of natural history to choose as a speciality. Probably the best advice for all naturalists is: *don't* specialise until you are familiar with a wide range of animals and

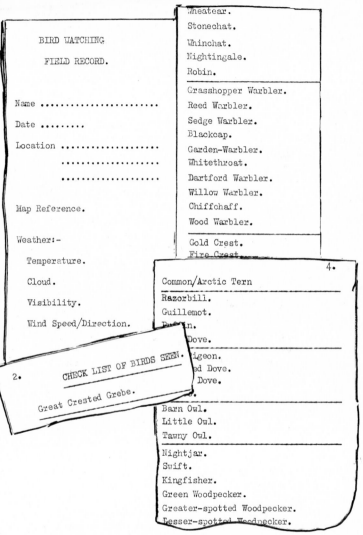

BIRD WATCHING

FIELD RECORD.

Name .....................

Date ........

Location ....................

....................

....................

Map Reference.

Weather:-

Temperature.

Cloud.

Visibility.

Wind Speed/Direction.

Wheatear.

Stonechat.

Whinchat.

Nightingale.

Robin.

Grasshopper Warbler.

Reed Warbler.

Sedge Warbler.

Blackcap.

Garden-Warbler.

Whitethroat.

Dartford Warbler.

Willow Warbler.

Chiffchaff.

Wood Warbler.

Gold Crest.

Fire Crest.

2.

CHECK LIST OF BIRDS SEEN.

Great Crested Grebe.

4.

Common/Arctic Tern

Razorbill.

Guillemot.

Puffin.

Dove.

Pigeon.

Dove.

Dove.

Barn Owl.

Little Owl.

Tawny Owl.

Nightjar.

Swift.

Kingfisher.

Green Woodpecker.

Greater-spotted Woodpecker.

Lesser-spotted Woodpecker.

20. A home-made pro-forma for regular use by a group of local birdwatchers

plants. The specialist who remains ignorant of other facets of natural history is missing a great deal of pleasure.

## Using the records

What are all these observations and notes for? Most naturalists are not satisfied to keep their findings to themselves. Around the country there are many natural history societies, and a large number of them produce newsletters and/or journals of some sort. Most of these accept not only weightier articles but also short 'fieldnotes', and individual species records. Indeed, editors usually welcome results derived from fieldwork. Writing an article (it need not be a formal scientific paper), or giving a talk to a local society, is a valuable outcome of the time spent in the field, and society recorders are always delighted to receive individual records (even if these are not formally written up as an article).

Local societies are not the only outlet for publicising discoveries. Many museum data banks are based mainly on amateurs' records (see Chapters 4 and 6). The regular transference of data from fieldnotes to the museum's files makes records available to a wider audience. There are also many national surveys to which the individual can contribute records (see Chapter 4).

The amateur can be of great help not only to other naturalists, but also to the general public. Considerable effort already goes into field surveys, the results of which are used by conservation organisations, local museum staff and planners, to assess the value of particular sites or habitats. It is surprising, and disappointing, how little is known in most parts of the country about, for instance, the richness of woodlands, the numbers of ponds and what they contain, or the most important wildlife refuges in urban areas. Many societies and nature conservation trusts have projects in which both experts and novices can participate. There is sure to be a controversial, or unworked site nearby, whether in town or country.

There is another way in which the naturalist can be of assistance to other people. More and more schools are carrying out field studies, and are making use of such sites as local parks, wasteland, or the school grounds themselves. Detailed information on such sites might be appreciated by teachers, if they do not have the time or expertise to gather it themselves. School natural history societies sometimes thrive on such doorstep projects.

## Types of projects

If you enjoy fieldwork you will probably be keen to start some sort of project, which may develop through a study of either a habitat or a taxonomic group of organisms. Probably the initial work on a study of a specific habitat, such as a wood or a pond, where a range of species will be discovered, some of their relationships can be studied, and the life cycles of several of them investigated.

In addition to a studying a single site in detail, a comparative survey of, for example, all the woods or areas of rough grassland over a wider area could be undertaken. This would provide much more variety, and would show something of the relationships between flora and fauna and soils, geology and topography. Especially interesting in such a project is an attempt to investigate the history of the locality using documents and archives, and the impact of land-use and management on the vegetation and the animal communities. From this could develop a survey of the area— for example, a tract of farmland which would gather information on all the habitats to be found. Such a study can be of considerable local value, if it is carried out systematically and thoroughly. This sort of survey is best undertaken by a group of people, each of whom has an expert interest, but an individual can easily tailor the study to suit his time and expertise.

The second type of project, and in a way the easier, is the concentrated study of one taxonomic group of plants or animals. Many people start their natural history studies with an interest in birds, or flowering plants, or butterflies. In the past, great emphasis was placed on collecting and preserving specimens of as many species and varieties as possible. Fortunately, this rather empty pursuit is much less popular now, and more naturalists are concerned to learn about the distributions, ecology and behaviour of their group, as well as its variations.

When starting to get to know a group it pays to choose one which is taxonomically not too difficult, which also means one which does not include a daunting number of species, and for which there are readily available identification manuals.

Although the scope for fieldwork in winter is certainly much more

limited than during the rest of the year a surprising number of
animals and some plants, notably mosses and liverworts, can be
observed in the depths of winter. A project which investigates
changes in an area throughout the year can be very rewarding.

Field projects need not be as general and extensive as the
suggestions made so far. They can be much more intensive studies.
What, for example, is the fate of the tree seedlings growing
underneath a woodland canopy? Are they the same species, and in
the same proportions, as the mature trees; and how long do they
survive? By marking out all areas, identifying, counting and
mapping all the seedlings in the sample area, and re-recording the
same area a couple of times a year, it is possible to see which are
likely to survive, and what variation there is in establishment success
from year to year.

Another project might involve the investigation of species of slugs
and snails in a particular area—their active periods and their feeding
habits. Regular observations, in wet and dry, warm and cool
weather, should provide interesting results.

Another assumption often made is that the amateur naturalist
should not experiment: that this is the preserve of 'real scientists'.
There are many experiments that anyone can carry out, which
require very little equipment and no special skills. The reading list at
the end of this chapter includes suggestions for projects and
investigations that can be carried out cheaply and easily and that
should be enjoyable to do.

## A project in the field
A useful exercise in observation and recording is the study of the
inhabitants—plant and animal—of a section of ordinary hedgerow.
If a diary is properly kept and comprehensive lists of species are
made, this type of study can have serious scientific value. There are
50–60 plant species, a large number of invertebrates, about 20 bird
species and several mammals that characteristically inhabit
hedgerows, so a wide cross-section of wildlife can be identified in a
year's work.

A study of the habits and relationships of all these organisms is
difficult, but an appreciation of their complexity can be a useful
experience as can be an awareness of the wider value of the

hedgerow in the landscape and its importance in connecting different woodland areas.

To focus more specifically on a single aspect of the hedgerow, observation of a single bramble shoot with a dozen ripe berries will reveal how dependent insects are on the fruit for food. After several days, plump shining black berries will be reduced to wizened folds of skin and stones. The frequency of wasp visits can be recorded, and their different methods of feeding. Wasps, for example, tear at the intact skins to get at the juices and once the skin is punctured the way is open for flies of various kinds. Each insect inserts its proboscis, pumps in saliva, and sucks out a mixture of saliva and partly digested pulp; the thin fluid thus created can be sipped out by the long, thin probe of a Speckled Wood butterfly. A host of other insects, not all connected with the bramble, for example greenbottle flies, midges, ichneumon flies and grasshoppers, may also be seen.

Inside some of the blackberries are the larvae of moths and beetles, originally laid as eggs in the flower heads. Some ichneumon flies locate these larvae in which to lay their own eggs, for they are parasites. Little is known about many of these host-parasite relationships and their study could reveal an interesting line of investigation.

The idea of relationships is more important. All living organisms are made from comparatively few interchangeable raw materials joined together in many different ways. These components are constantly circulated between organisms. Thus the observation of a single blackberry shoot can show the complexity of the build-up and decay, and the process of ecological balance; and the picture is seen to be far more detailed than was first thought.

Insects are not the only feeders on the blackberries. Footprints in the soil show where badgers and foxes have visited the bramble patch; and in a wood, the droppings in the badger dirt pit may glisten with drying blackberry pips. The badger droppings have their own population of worms, mites, larvae and beetles, and a fungal succession which can be revealed by keeping the droppings in a warm place under a glass cover. On hedgerow leaves and stems, further blackberry pips stick out from a froth of purple mucus left by blackbirds, which poses some interesting thoughts on the process of seed dispersal.

All these observations are worth recording, and notes on the fragments of relationships can be the starting point for further speculations. For example, it might be questioned whether the pips that have passed through the badger have died, or whether they will still germinate? If so, will they germinate more quickly than dry pips which have fallen to the ground? By collecting pips from both sources, then planting equal numbers of them in sterile compost, and treating the samples alike, it is possible to find out.

This part in the question process is the stage of *experiment*, and the trying out of a *hypothesis*. It is no exaggeration to say that a whole book waits to be written about those few blackberries and their relationships. Feeding, reproduction, survival and adaptive behaviour, the most fundamental biological processes, are all bound up in these intricate relationships.

Fieldwork can be enjoyed and valued for itself, but it is much more useful if conclusions are drawn from it at intervals, and further lines of study tested out. The criticism and encouragement of others working in the same field is necessary, and this is one reason why it is so important to join local and national societies and so meet other naturalists.

## Basic field equipment

Finally what equipment should the naturalist have? Some things are essential and obvious; others depend on one's personal bent; and there are many luxuries or sophisticated items available.

Anyone who takes natural history seriously needs good quality, warm, weatherproof, sombre-coloured and quiet-sounding, soilable **clothing**, and strong, waterproof **footgear**. Jackets or anoraks should have (or can be altered to have) several pockets, at least one large enough to take a map and notebook. Boots are less tiring than wellingtons, and if properly cared for will allow a certain amount of paddling.

A **backpack**, again of a sombre colour, will be needed for spare clothing, food, field equipment and specimens. A very large pack can be more of an inconvenience than an asset—but remember that naturalists inevitably return home carrying more than they set out with! Select a pack with wide, comfortable shoulder-straps and one or more pockets. If you need a large pack, choose one with a frame:

the comfort is well worth the cost. Packs are rarely waterproof, so it is a good idea to line your pack with a large polythene bag. Wet specimens should always be carefully separated from the other contents of the bag. What goes into the pack depends largely on personal preference, but should include a notebook and pencil and spare paper.

Most naturalists use **binoculars**, if only for viewing the scenery. Binoculars are expensive items, and although many of the modern glasses are very good value for money, it is sensible to seek advice before buying a pair. The Royal Society for the Protection of Birds and the British Trust for Ornithology both issue helpful booklets. Points to look for are:

1. Centre-wheel focusing, and smooth movement of all parts.

2. Lens diameter should give a light-gathering power factor of at least 4. Thus an 8 (magnification) × 40 mm (lens diameter) formula means that the light gathering factor $= \dfrac{\text{lens diameter}}{\text{magnification}}$ $= \dfrac{40}{8} = 5$, which is good. Light gathering power is more important than magnification, for most purposes. Some common formulae are: 6 × 30 (rather low power); 8 × 30, 8 × 40, 7 × 50, (all generally useful); 10 × 50 (large and heavy); 12 × 50 (needs a tripod mount).

3. Lenses should be 'bloomed' i.e. appear blue or orange against the light.

4. Binoculars should be light in weight, fit the hands well, and be comfortable against the eyes or spectacles.

5. The field of view should be wide, for example at least 7°(120 m at 1 000 m) for an 8 × 40 glass.

6. When focused centrally on a clear object such as a pole, the image should be sharp over most of the lens when the glasses are moved from side to side, and no 'rainbow' colours should appear at the edge of the picture.

As binoculars are valuable, it may be advisable to insure them against damage. Some naturalists prefer to use a telescope, especially for distant bird or deer watching, but for general purposes they are not recommended.

Most naturalists also use—or should use—a **hand lens**. The most useful is of × 10 magnification, folding into a metal, rather than plastic, casing. A higher magnification is of little use to the beginner. If the lens is likely to be in frequent use, carry it on a neck-cord.

A variety of **containers** is another requisite, although as has been stressed, collecting should be kept to the minimum. A few polythene bags and a rectangular, watertight, food box cater for most needs. Tobacco tins are very useful for small specimens, but they are inclined to rattle. Each container should be properly identified with **labels**. The best method is to number each bag and box with indelible ink before setting out, and to refer to these numbers in your field notes. In addition, put a label inside each container with the specimen. The back pages of your notebook, or separate small pieces of paper, will supply the labels.

Much natural history is now done with a **camera**. For general work little compares with a single lens 35 mm reflex camera with interchangeable lenses and a set of extension tubes. Cameras can be very good value secondhand, if examined and tried out by an expert. (The local photographic society can usually supply such a person). Praktika, Pentax, and Zenith cameras have interchangeable lenses and accessories, so that once you buy a camera body you have access to an enormous range of equipment to fit it. Other makers tend to fit their own exclusive range.

The advantage of a single lens reflex camera is simply that the picture it takes is an exact reflection of what is focused through— there are no parallax errors to worry about. The addition of inexpensive tubes between the camera body and the lens will enable you to focus the picture as little as 5 cm away. The camera is an important tool for many naturalists and a demonstration session in the field is the best way to acquire the necessary basic knowledge to use it successfully.

**Ordnance survey maps** are the only ones suitable for most naturalists' fieldwork. The most useful are the 1:25 000 scale sheets, which show field boundaries. Each, however, covers only 100 km, so a naturalist's normal fieldwork range should be covered also by 1:50 000 sheets. Maps are best protected by stout polythene bags. A **compass** will be necessary for such work as detailed mapping. However, compasses can lead to trouble: the novice should not use one for navigation without training. In order to carry out mapping work, a **survey tape** may be needed. For smaller scale work, a 2 m retractable steel tape or a tailor's cloth tape can be invaluable, and should be routinely carried.

**Nets** seem to be somewhat out of favour, but anyone indulging in freshwater or marine natural history will often need one. Nets for catching or sampling insects may also be required. Specialist books and catalogues should be consulted before buying these items. Remember that tough hessian is used for sea and pond dipping, and that although a large, loose fine-mesh net is needed for much work with insects, a stronger net is needed for 'sweeping' vegetation.

The geologist needs a special **hammer**, and hard chisels; both he and other naturalists may also wish to carry a narrow fern or bulb **trowel** for extracting specimens from crevices or for digging. A **sheath knife** is also excellent for these jobs. All these, however, need to be used with care and constraint, remembering that damage caused during the collection of a specimen is usually more serious than the removal of the specimen itself.

Any naturalist should always carry a strong **pocket-knife**; and, of course, several lengths of string. **Trays**, white **polythene sheets** and even upturned umbrellas can be used to collect the specimens that result from the vigorous beating of foliage for sampling invertebrate populations.

## More specialized equipment

Once a naturalist becomes involved in specialized studies a wide range of equipment becomes important and the items described in this section are the most frequently used. A list of suppliers is given at the end of this chapter.

For measuring micro-climatic conditions **simple thermometers**, **soil thermometers**, wet and dry bulb, hair or paper **hygrometers**, and simple **wind strength indicators** can all be obtained from specialist dealers. These items are small enough to be carried in a pocket if necessary. In the field an indication of soil acidity (pH value) can be obtained by using **BDH pocket kits** which can be bought from garden shops.

Sudbury Soils Ltd., Upper Birchetts, Langton Green, Tunbridge Wells, Kent, supply a booklet with details of more complicated testing outfits.

For detailed vegetation mapping, inexpensive **survey poles** can be made from garden canes with ends split to hold a small card, and painted in contrasting 20 cm bands. Collapsible **quadrat squares** can be made from aluminium or wood strips, or string pegged at the corners. The traditional metre square is too big for much general use; the 50 × 50 cm square is often more convenient. A smaller homemade, wooden 25 × 25 cm square, subdivided with nylon fishing line, can be the most useful of all. It fits into a rucksack easily, and can be used for sampling barnacles, lichens, and for many other purposes.

**Sieves** made from bottomless seed boxes, covered with $\frac{1}{4}$ inch (6 mm) wire mesh or perforated zinc are useful for rough examination of soil or litter. Sets of soil sieves of known mesh are available through dealers. A **hand counter** is useful for sampling colonies, for example of rook nests in a rookery; seabirds passing a given point on a cliff; or plant species growing in a sample area.

A field or botanical **press** is easily made from 5-plyboards, held together with strong clips or straps or buckles. Alternate layers of newspapers and clean kitchen paper (all unglazed) enable specimens to be laid flat, and for the drying process to be started in the field. A similar, but larger press, on which increasing weights can be put, can be used at home. Certain fresh material can be fixed to cards in the field with Takibak or similar self-adhesive transparent plastic.

For catching moths at night a **mercury vapour lamp** will be needed and for extracting soil organisms a **Berlese funnel** is useful.

The best way to become familiar with the use of all field equipment is to go on an appropriate course at one of the Field Studies Centres (see Chapter 5) or to undertake fieldwork with an experienced member of a natural history society on a regular basis. Equipment can be used and tried out before it is purchased, and expert advice is available.

It may seem trite to end with cautionary notes; however, the fieldworker's pack, wherever the work is, should always contain a little **food**: chocolate is traditional, and good for emergency needs. In hill areas, take a **whistle** in case help is needed; and in these areas you should also carry a **torch** and enough **protective clothing** to enable you to survive an overnight stranding. Finally, *wherever* you are working in the field, someone responsible should be given the details of your likely route and latest anticipated return time.

## List of suppliers

Airflow Developments Ltd
Lancaster Road
High Wycombe
Bucks HP12 3QP

Meteorological
equipment

Casella London Ltd
Regent House
Britannia Walk
London N1 7ND

Meteorological
equipment

L. Christie
129 Franciscan Road
Tooting
London SW17 8DZ

Entomological
equipment

The Clarkson Group
1 Brixton Hill Place
London SW2 1HL

Surveying equipment

Cutrock Engineering Co. Ltd
Rowlen House
272 Abbeydale Road
Wembley
Middx N3 IXL

Geological hammers and
soil augers

Grant Instruments (Cambridge) Ltd
Barrington
Cambridge CB2 5QZ

Portable temperature
recorder and probes

T. Gerrard & Co
Gerrard House
Worthing Road
East Preston
West Sussex BN16 1AS

General to schools,
colleges, societies
and individuals with
accounts only

Griffin & George Ltd
PO Box 11
Ledson Road
Wythenshawe
Manchester M23 9NP

Wide range of surveying, meteorological and portable measuring instruments. Nets, compasses, geological hammers and specimen tubes and bottles.

Philip Harris Ltd
Lynn Lane
Shenstone
Staffs WS14 0EE

(As above)

Heron Optics
23–25 Kings Road
Brentwood
Essex CM14 4ER

Binoculars, telescopes, climbing equipment and clothing.

Ordnance Survey
Romsey Road
Maybush
Southampton SO9 4DH

Maps

Survey and General Instrument Co
Fircroft Way
Edenbridge
Kent TN8 6HA

Surveying equipment and stereoscopes

Watkins & Doncaster
Four Throws
Hawkhurst
Kent TN18 5ED

Entomological

**Further reading**

This list should be used in conjunction with those books listed at the end of Chapter 2.

Arnold, N. 1976. *Wildlife conservation by young people*. London: Ward Lock.

Arnold, N. 1978. *The young naturalist's guide to conservation.* London: Ward Lock.

Chinery, M. 1977. *The family naturalist.* London: Macdonald and Janes.

Corbet, G. B. 1975. *Finding and identifying mammals in Britain.* London: British Museum (Natural History).

Dennis, E. (ed.) 1972. *Everyman's nature reserve. Ideas for action.* Newton Abbot: David and Charles.

Devon Trust for Nature Conservation (ed.) 1972. *School projects in natural history.* London: Heinemann Educational Books.

Durman, R. (ed.) 1976. *Bird observatories in Britain and Ireland.* Berkhamsted: Poyser.

Ellis, E. A. 1975. *The countryside in autumn. The countryside in spring. The countryside in winter. The countryside in summer.* Norwich: Jarrold. (four title series.)

Falkus, H. 1978. *A nature detective.* London: Gollancz.

Ford, R. L. E. 1973. *Studying insects, a practical guide.* London: Warne.

Gilpin, A. 1977. *Know the game: birdwatching.* Wakefield: EP Publishing.

Gilpin, A. 1978. *Nature photography.* Wakefield: EP Publishing.

Gooders, J. 1975. *How to watch birds.* London: Andre Deutsch.

Lewis, T. & Taylor, L. R. 1967. *Introduction to experimental ecology.* London: Academic Press.

Nuridsany, C. & Perennov, M. 1976. *Photographing nature.* London: Kaye & Ward.

Owen, D. 1978. *Town and gardens.* Sevenoaks: Hodder & Stoughton.

Philips, R. 1978. *Watching wildlife.* London: Knight.

Soper, T. 1978. *Wildlife begins at home.* London: Pan.

Teagle, W. G. 1978. *The endless village. The wildlife of Birmingham, Dudley, Sandwell, Walsall, and Wolverhampton.* Shrewsbury: Nature Conservancy Council.

Watson, G. G. 1971. *Fun with ecology.* rev. edn. London: Kaye and Ward.

# 4. Biological recording

J. Heath and P. T. Harding

Naturalists have been interested in the occurrence of the flora and fauna of Britain and Ireland since at least the seventeenth century (Allen, 1976), and their study of it, and particularly of distributions, has caught the imagination and enthusiasm of many, both amateur and professional. The Biological Records Centre (BRC) at the Monks Wood Experimental Station of the Institute of Terrestrial Ecology has been developing a role to service recording schemes for the British Isles.

The Biological Records Centre was set up in 1964 by Dr. F. H. Perring after the completion of the Botanical Society of the British Isles' (BSBI) survey of the vascular plant flora (Perring & Walters, 1962). The techniques of recording, data handling and data use, pioneered by the BSBI, were applied to several other groups of organisms. As data handling technology has been advanced and the wider potential of the recording scheme principles has been realized, many more groups have been covered by national recording schemes.

## National recording schemes

Each recording scheme differs in some way from the rest, but in essence each attempts to organize naturalists who are willing to contribute records to submit them in a standard form. The simplest type of record is of a species at a locality (identified by a national grid reference and usually by a place name), on a date, recorded by a named individual.

The pioneer scheme was that of the BSBI, for vascular plants, begun in 1954. This scheme, as proposed by Professor A. R. Clapham, was to record the presence of plants in the 10 km. squares of the national grid, rather than in the more usual but much larger Watson/Praeger vice-counties, or by localities as had been done by some continental workers. Many of the records received by the BSBI scheme were summarized in the form of records for a 10 km. square. The limited usefulness of such summarized records was soon realized by the BRC and other recording schemes were eventually encouraged to record in detail and then to summarize the data at a later date.

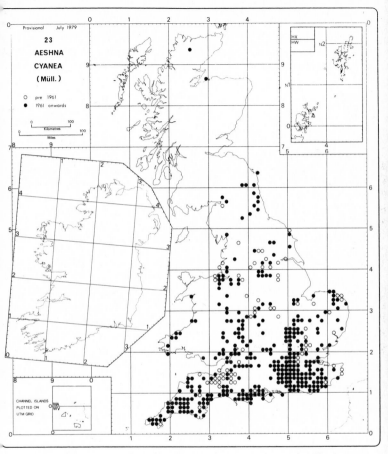

Provisional    July 1979

**23**

**AESHNA**

**CYANEA**

**( Müll. )**

○   pre 1961

●   1961 onwards

CHANNEL ISLANDS
PLOTTED ON
UTM GRID

21. Map showing distribution of the Southern Aeshna (dragonfly), produced by the Biological Records Centre

Each scheme has at least one central organizer responsible for the gathering of records from naturalists or from regional organizers dealing directly with the naturalists in their area. Many of these recording schemes have been set up and are run by 'amateur' societies or by private individuals. Others are run as projects by individuals at academic or research organizations or in museums.

## The role of the Biological Records Centre

BRC acts as a focus for the recording schemes and as a depository for data collected by them, to form a national data bank and archive of the occurrence of the flora and fauna in the British Isles.

The organizers of national recording schemes are helped with advice on the setting up and operation of their schemes, with the provision of recording cards and other stationery, with means of publicizing their schemes, and instructions for recorders (Heath & Scott, 1977).

Once sufficient data have been accumulated by a scheme they are deposited with BRC, in the national biological data bank. Once deposited, distribution maps can be prepared, and it is these maps that most recording scheme organizers see as their main objective. It is usual for preliminary or provisional distribution maps to be produced and made available to the contributors to the relevant scheme.

Output from the data bank can be in the form of the now well known 10 km. Square 'dot' distribution maps (ill. 21) or listings of species for localities or of localities for species. The data are also available for use in analyses in conjunction with other data sets, such as of environmental factors. This aspect of the use of the BRC data bank is currently being developed within the Institute.

The data bank exists in two forms: summarized data are stored on the IBM 360/195 computer at the Rutherford Laboratory; the 'raw' data, usually on one of three types of recording card, from which the summaries were made, are stored by taxonomic groups and arranged by 10 km. squares in card drawers at BRC.

Data can be made available on request to any serious enquirer, subject to some obvious restrictions, e.g. on data for rare and endangered species, or where the data will be exploited for commercial gain. Occasionally BRC receives enquiries or requests for information which are impractical because the enquirers are unaware of the quantity or quality of data involved or the complexity of their enquiry.

The BRC has a special relationship with the Nature Conservancy

Council and supplies it with information, particularly on the occurrence of rare and endangered species, which can be used in planning the nation's official policy for wildlife conservation. Voluntary conservation bodies such as Nature Conservation Trusts and their 'parent body', The Society for the Promotion of Nature Conservation, local biological records centres and national and local natural history societies all enjoy useful collaboration with BRC.

Input on the British flora and fauna to various international surveys is made through BRC, including the Atlas Florae Europeae project and the European Invertebrate Survey.

## Other forms of recording

It would be unrealistic to infer that biological recording does not exist in Britain without the involvement of the national recording schemes and/or the BRC. Most data coming to BRC have a bias to geographical occurrence; comparatively few data are available on the habitats of species. This work, mainly by amateur naturalists, on geographical distribution supplements autecological research at academic and research organizations. However, the lengthy and labour-intensive studies of single species can necessarily only cover a limited number of species, whereas national recording schemes are often able to draw upon large numbers of recorders. For example, between 1968 and 1972 over 10 000 ornithologists provided records of the birds breeding in Britain and Ireland in a survey organized by the British Trust for Ornithology and the Irish Wildbird Conservancy (Sharrock, 1976).

Although data from the national recording schemes are available to research workers wishing to make autecological studies, in some cases the results of neither a national recording scheme nor autecological studies can answer a particular problem. In such a case a special survey has to be set up. The butterfly monitoring scheme (Pollard, 1979) seeks to examine the fluctuations in numbers of butterflies at a number of localities by regular and systematic sampling (by observation). The British Trust for Ornithology has organized several special national surveys of birds and their habitats, one of which was the 'Common Birds Census' (Williamson & Homes, 1964). Schemes were set up for some invertebrate groups, about which very little was known, to examine their habitat preferences *and* geographical distribution (Barber & Fairhurst, 1974). Also within the Institute of Terrestrial Ecology the Phytophagous Insect Data Bank provides information, mainly derived from published sources, on phytophagous insects and their food-plants.

**Further information**
Details of the national recording schemes and their organizers, of atlases of distribution maps and of local records centres are available on request from:

Biological Records Centre
Institute of Terrestrial Ecology
Monks Wood Experimental Station
Abbots Ripton
Huntingdon
PE17 2LS

**References**

Allen, D. E. 1976. *the naturalist in Britain a social history*. London: Allen Lane.

Barber, A. D. & Fairhurst, C. P. 1974. A habitat and distribution recording scheme for Myriapoda and other invertebrates. *Symp. Zool. Soc. Lond.* **32**, 611–619.

Heath, J. & Scott, D. 1977. *Biological Records Centre—Instructions for recorders*. Huntingdon: Biological Records Centre.

Perring, F. H. & Walters, S. M. 1962. *Atlas of the British flora*. London: Nelson, for the Botanical Society of the British Isles.

Pollard, E. 1979. A national scheme for monitoring the abundance of butterflies: the first three years. *Proc. Brit. ent. Nat. Hist. Soc.* **12**, 77–90.

Sharrock, J. T. R. 1976. *The Atlas of breeding birds in Britain and Ireland*. Berkhamsted: Poyser, for the British Trust for Ornithology and the Irish Wildbird Conservancy.

Williamson, K. & Homes, R. C. 1964. Methods and preliminary results of the common birds census, 1962–63. *Bird Study*, **11**, 240–256.

## Vice-counties and grid references
Details of the Watsonian vice-county and National Grid systems for recording the distribution of plants and animals in the British Isles are to be found in appendices A and B (pages 191–196).

## Atlases of the fauna and flora of the British Isles
The following are available from Biological Records Centre, Institute of Terrestrial Ecology, Monks Wood Experimental Station, Abbots Ripton, Huntingdon PE17 2LS.

PTERIDOPHYTES
*Atlas of ferns of the British Isles*, 1978, editors A. C. Jermy, H. R. Arnold, L. Farrell & F. H. Perring.

BRYOPHYTES
*Provisional atlas of the bryophytes of the British Isles* 1978, editor A. J. E. Smith (104 species).

AMPHIBIANS and REPTILES
*Provisional atlas of the amphibians and reptiles of the British Isles*, 1973, editor H. R. Arnold.

MAMMALS
*Provisional atlas of the mammals of the British Isles,* 1978, editor H. R. Arnold.

INSECTS
*Provisional atlas of the insects of the British Isles*
Part 1. *Lepidoptera: Rhopalocera (Butterflies)*, 1970, editor J. Heath. OUT OF PRINT.
Part 2. *Lepidoptera: Sphingidae, Notodontidae, Lymantriidae, Lasiocampidae, Saturniidae, Endromidae, Drepanidae, Arctiidae, Nolidae and Thyatiridae (Moths part 1)* (101 species), 1973, editors J. Heath & M. J. Skelton. OUT OF PRINT.
Part 3. *Hymenoptera: Apidae (Bumblebees)*, 1973, editor D. V. Alford. OUT OF PRINT.
Part 4. *Siphonaptera (Fleas)*, 1974, editor R. S. George.

Part 5. *Hymenoptera: Formicidae (Ants)*, 2nd edition 1979, editor
K. E. J. Barrett.
Part 6. *Orthoptera (Grasshoppers & crickets)*. 2nd edition 1979,
editor E. C. M. Haes.
Part 7. *Odonata (Dragonflies)*, 2nd edition 1979, editor D. G.
Chelmick.
Part 8. *Trichoptera: Hydroptilidae (Caddisflies, part 1)*, 1978, editor
J. E. Marshall.
Part 9. *Hymenoptera: Vespidae (Social wasps)*, 2nd edition 1979,
editor M. E. Archer.
*Atlas of the bumblebees of the British Isles*, 1980.


MOLLUSCS
*Atlas of the non-marine mollusca of the British Isles*, 1976, editor
M. P. Kerney.


CRUSTACEANS
*Provisional atlas of the crustacea of the British Isles*. Part 1, *Isopoda:
Oniscoidea (Woodlice)*, 1976, editor P. T. Harding.


NEMATODES
*Provisional atlas of the nematodes of the British Isles*. Parts 1–3,
*Longidoridae, Trichodoridae and Criconematidae*. 1977, editors
D. J. F. Brown, C. E. Taylor, B. Boag, T. J. W. Alphey and K. J.
Orton Williams.


OVERLAYS OF ENVIRONMENTAL FACTORS
*Overlays of environmental and other factors for use with Biological
Records Centre distribution maps*, 1978.
Contains: Altitude, Geology (chalk and limestone), Rivers, Upland
moorland, Western oakwoods, February minimum temperature,
January mean temperature, July mean temperature, Annual rainfall,
Wet days, Vice-county boundaries, County boundaries.

# 5. Field centres

Henry Disney

The significant increase in the number of field centres in Britain has been one of the more noticeable developments in natural history education over the past thirty years. Although this development was largely stimulated by the example of the Council for the Promotion of Field Studies (now called the Field Studies Council), most field centres are now run by Local Education Authorities. Although the latter outnumber all other field centres combined, they sometimes cater only for schoolchildren.

The adult amateur or student wishing to study a special topic may therefore have to consider a field centre under some other sponsorship. The Youth Hostels Association, for example, has played an important part in providing facilities for field studies. More detailed information on field centres can be found in *A directory of field centres in England and Wales* (available from the Council for Environmental Education, School of Education, University of Reading, Reading, Berkshire, RG1 5AG). Information on field centres in Scotland can be obtained from the Scottish Field Studies Association (Kindrogan Field Centre, Enochdhu, Blairgowrie, Perth, PH10 7BG). The National Institute of Adult Education (19B De Montford Street, Leicester, LE1 7GE) publishes a six-monthly calendar of residential short courses that includes courses at Field Centres for amateur naturalists.

The concept of the field centre brings together three concerns: first and historically the earliest, was the desire to extend the traditional naturalist's guided walk for a longer period of time; second, was the desire of teachers to give their students actual experience of nature in the field as opposed to the classroom; third, conservationists wanted to propagate their gospel of concern for the environment on the basis of first-hand experience.

For many years specialists in various aspects of British natural history have led parties of amateurs on guided walks, the intention being that the participants should have an enjoyable outing, learn from the expertise of their leader and capture something of his enthusiasm. This tradition is still a major feature of local natural history societies, and when well done can provide a most exhilarating and educational experience.

The second development was the desire to take schoolchildren and students from established educational institutions into the field for periods longer than the customary half-day excursion. Undergraduates from Oxford and Cambridge have been attending field courses at marine biology stations such as that of the Marine Biological Association at Plymouth for at least a hundred years. Most higher education institutions providing study courses on biology, geography and related subjects utilize field centres, and some universities run their own field stations.

Until very recently the emphasis of the courses was on methods of identification, collecting and training in practical taxonomy. During the 1940s there was a movement towards the provision of wider facilities for fieldwork in order to make use of the environment as a springboard for laboratory and classroom based studies in schools.

The third development, which provided both the impetus and justification for the field centre movement, was the growing awareness of the need for conservation. This increasing concern for the environment coincided with an upsurge of demand by educationalists that the study of science (and other disciplines) should be more relevant to the concerns of contemporary society. There is no doubt that the high quality of the teaching at so many field centres springs from a genuine commitment to the conservation movement.

Field courses can be classified according to their method of organization: first, there are those run by field centre staff as part of the centre's normal programme; second, there are supplementary courses taken by outside specialists. This practice enables a field centre to offer a range of courses extending far beyond the expertise of its own staff.

Special courses may also be commissioned by a school, college, natural history society, or other organization. A special example of this was the request by the Open University for the Field Studies Council to run summer schools for their ecology courses; several centres are now involved in providing this service.

Some institutions or natural history societies may decide to run their own course at a field centre in consultation with field centre staff. Some students may attend a field course in order to further a definite educational aim while others prefer to pursue a private

22a. Kindrogan Field Centre, Perthshire
22b. Malham Tarn Field Centre, West Yorkshire

interest. Those who use the field centre primarily as a holiday base can draw on the advice of the centre staff for information on walks, good sites for bird-watching etc. and will value the centre's facilities, such as the library and laboratory space, as well as the field centre atmosphere.

As has been pointed out by Sinker (1967), the basic requirements of anyone wishing to run a field course are a residential base from which to operate, working sites that are attractive in terms of the studies it is proposed to undertake, security of access to these chosen working sites, indoor working space together with the necessary books and apparatus—sometimes of a sophisticated nature—and, in addition, a fund of local background information and technical advice on which to draw.

A wide range of subjects is offered at field centres throughout Britain. For example, table 1, p. 94 presents an analysis of the types of course offered for sixth-form students by the nine residential field centres of the Field Studies Council in 1977; these can be compared with an analysis of courses offered to adults in the same year (see table 2, p. 95).

The extraordinary popularity of birds compared with invertebrates, or flowering plants compared with lower plants, is evident from this table. Furthermore, the aesthetic response to the natural world is highlighted by the courses on drawing, painting and photography. The large category 'miscellaneous' conceals the full range of subjects studied at field centres, as a random selection of courses indicates—Wildlife Sound Recording, Winemaking, Natural Gardening and Self-sufficiency, Cycling in Shropshire and the Borderlands, Landscape into Enamel, and Geology and Gemstones.

There is also a great variation in the level at which courses are pitched. For example, a course entitled 'Small Creatures' attempts to introduce the novice to the variety of invertebrates and how to use keys and microscopes to identify them; whereas a course entitled 'Flies, Midges and Gnats' assumes some knowledge of insects and familiarity with keys, and is aimed at those wishing to learn about one particular order in more detail.

It is this provision of courses for students at different levels of knowledge and attainment that has enabled field centres to help novices to become amateur specialists of distinction in their field.

For instance, many amateurs, who first acquired their expertise at a field centre, are now contributing valuable records to the mapping schemes co-ordinated by the Biological Records Centre (see Chapter 4).

There is no doubt that field centres have played an important role in overcoming the amateur's awe of scientific natural history, to the point where he can contribute on equal terms with the professional. If there was no other justification for field centres then this would go a long way towards providing one.

In 1959, the journal *Field Studies* was established by the Field Studies Council to provide a vehicle for the publication of papers about aspects of the environments in which the field centres are situated. It was decided as a matter of editorial policy that even the most specialized contributions to the journal should be written in a generally comprehensible style.

Areas around field centres are now becoming surprisingly well documented, particularly the nature reserves and adjacent landscapes at the Malham Tarn and Slapton Ley Field Centres. Contributions relating to the Malham Tarn Field Centre (opened in 1947) that have appeared in *Field Studies* have covered many aspects of the fauna, flora, geology, archaeology, agriculture etc. (e.g. Clayton 1966; Disney 1975; Duffey 1963; Holmes 1960; Lund 1961; Manley 1957; O'Connor 1964; Pigott & Pigott 1959; Proctor 1960, 1974; Raistrick & Gilbert 1963; Raistrick & Holmes 1962; Sinker 1960). Many other Field Centres can boast a similar output of publications.

A remarkable development at the Orielton Field Centre in Wales has been the creation of the Oil Pollution Research Unit. This is now a more or less autonomous research unit with an international reputation in the field of monitoring the effects of pollutants from the oil industry on marine and estuarine ecosystems (Carthy and Arthur 1968).

Apart from published documentation in *Field Studies* and elsewhere, most field centres have valuable unpublished records. These cover such information as meteorological data, detailed hydrological records for stream catchments, or records of vegetational changes in mown and unmown plots. The resident staff are often able to explain anomalies because they have witnessed and recorded unusual events, like a storm shifting a shingle ridge or fire destroying part of a heath. This local knowledge is an important asset at an established field centre.

No less striking is the output of drawings, paintings, photographs and other artistic records of these environments. In the case of Flatford Mill Field Centre in Suffolk the association with John Constable has attracted numerous aspiring artists. Not only have artists and scientists generally benefited by rubbing shoulders with each other at a field centre, but there have been a series of courses that have deliberately brought the two together. There are courses on Botanical Illustration, in which students are encouraged to combine botanical accuracy with artistic excellence, and courses that start from scientific description and explanation and proceed to artistic design and inspiration. This sharing of the viewpoints of scientist and artist has been more meaningfully, and less self-consciously achieved at field centres than almost anywhere else one could name.

The many ways in which the natural world is viewed is perhaps the most striking feature of the field centre's activity and behind this diversification is a unifying appreciation of, and concern for, the environment.

**References**

Carthy, J. D. & Arthur, D. R. (eds.) 1968. The biological effects of oil pollution on littoral communities. *Field Studies* **2** (Suppl.), 1–198.

Clayton, K. M. 1966. The origin of the landforms of the Malham area. *Field Studies* **2**, 359–84.

Disney, R. H. L. 1975. Review of management policy for the Malham Tarn estate. *Field Studies* **4**, 223–42.

Duffey, E. 1963. Ecological studies on the spider fauna of the Malham Tarn area. *Field Studies* **1**, 65–87.

Herbert, A. T., Oswald, P. H. & Sinker, C. A. 1972. Centres for field studies in England and Wales: the results of a questionnaire survey in 1969. *Field Studies* **3**, 665–79.

Holmes, P. F. 1960. The birds of Malham Moor. *Field Studies* **1**, 49–60.

Lund, J. W. G. 1961. The algae of the Malham Tarn district. *Field Studies* **1**, 85–119.

Manley, G. 1957. The climate at Malham Tarn. *Field Studies Council Annual Report* 1955–1956, 43–56.

O'Connor, J. 1964. The geology of the area around Malham Tarn, Yorkshire. *Field Studies* **2**, 53–82.

Pigott, M. E. & Pigott, C. D. 1959. Stratigraphy and pollen analysis of Malham Tarn and Tarn Moss. *Field Studies* **1**, 84–101.

Proctor, M. C. F. 1960. Mosses and liverworts of the Malham district. *Field Studies* **1**, 61–85.

Proctor, M. C. F. 1974. The vegetation of the Malham Tarn fens. *Field Studies* **4**, 1–38.

Raistrick, A. & Gilbert, O. L. 1963. Malham Tarn House: its building materials, their weathering and colonization by plants. *Field Studies* **1**, 89–115.

Raistrick, A. & Holmes, P. F. 1962. Archaeology of Malham Moor. *Field Studies* **1**, 73–100.

Sinker, C. A. 1960. The vegetation of the Malham Tarn area. *Proceedings of the Leeds Philosophical and Literary Society, Science Section* **8** (5), 1–37.

Sinker, C. A. 1967. The role of field centres in ecological teaching. In *The teaching of ecology* (ed. J. M. Lambert) pp. 221–228. Oxford: Blackwell.

TABLE 1

The variety of courses designed for sixth-form students that were advertized by the nine residential field centres of the Field Studies Council in 1977. Figures are percentages of total courses. (Courses at the non-residential Epping Forest Conservation Centre, High Beach, Loughton, Essex, are not included.)

| Subject | % |
| --- | --- |
| Geography | 40.8 |
| Ecology | 30.5 |
| Marine ecology | 13.5 |
| Geology | 4.9 |
| Freshwater ecology | 4.9 |
| Geomorphology | 2.0 |
| Zoology | 1.9 |
| Environmental studies | 0.6 |
| Biogeography | 0.6 |
| Botany | 0.2 |
| Conservation | 0.1 |

TABLE 2

A synopsis of the variety of courses for adults advertised by the
Field Studies Council in 1977. Figures are percentages of total
courses. (Details of current courses may be obtained from The
Information Office, The Field Studies Council, Preston Montford,
Montford Bridge, Shrewsbury SY4 1HW.)

| Subject | % |
|---|---|
| Exploration of landscape, geology, scenery, etc. | 17.0 |
| Birds | 10.6 |
| Painting, drawing, illustrating, etc. | 9.6 |
| Ecology, special habitats, etc. | 7.9 |
| General natural history | 7.6 |
| Flowering plants | 6.3 |
| Environmental studies, man and landscape, etc. | 6.0 |
| Photography | 5.0 |
| Architecture | 4.0 |
| Lower plants | 3.9 |
| Courses for A-level teachers | 3.3 |
| Invertebrates | 3.3 |
| Mammals | 1.9 |
| Marine biology for divers | 1.6 |
| Meteorology | 1.3 |
| Rocks, fossils, minerals, etc. | 1.3 |
| Conservation | 1.0 |
| Archaeology | 0.9 |
| Miscellaneous | 7.5 |

# 6. Natural history museums

Frank H. Brightman

Great Britain is quite well provided with museums, and public galleries of some kind or another are found in most towns. The main emphasis is frequently either on archaeology and local history, or else on the arts, especially painting. However, there are about 200 museums which display at least some natural history exhibits and possess relevant collections of some kind. Even the most modest of them are worth a visit. Amateur naturalists can learn much in museums; and equally important, because of their special interests and knowledge, they can help in a number of ways to make the displays and collections more useful to others.

The big national museums may seem vast on first acquaintance and appear to be rather overwhelming. On the other hand, in the smaller local museums the exhibits may consist of little more than a few mounted skins of birds and mammals, but it should be remembered that although storage space never seems to be fully adequate even in large museums, exhibition space is usually even more restricted, and therefore the reserve collections are always worth enquiring about. They may include more or less comprehensive collections of a particular group of animals, dried and pressed plants, or specimens of fossils, rocks and minerals. Such collections were usually acquired by the museum in the first place as gifts or bequests from the original collectors, and may or may not have been augmented later by the efforts of the museum staff and others. If they were mainly made by a single collector the personality and idiosyncrasies of the individual are often apparent, which may add some historical interest, but which unfortunately frequently limits their general value from a purely natural history point of view.

Comprehensive collections of specimens of a particular group, or from a particular locality or area, are what interest most naturalists today. Collections, made more or less at random, of the largest, the most spectacular and the rarest specimens, and omitting the commoner but not necessarily less interesting ones, stimulate merely a passing curiosity rather than a sustained interest.

## Museum displays

The policy of most museums used to be to put as much of the collections on display as possible. There is much to be said in favour of this policy when a collection is reasonably comprehensive as, for instance, when specimens of all the commoner birds of the neighbourhood (ill. 23) or a nearly complete series of fossils from a particular geological exposure can be exhibited. Nevertheless crowded cases and brief factual labels attract only those visitors who are quite well initiated into natural history studies.

23. A fine example of a diorama, at Colchester Natural History Museum. It shows the Colne Estuary at Fingringhoe Wick, with Brent Geese in the foreground

More recently, in order to appeal to a broader section of the public, many curators have adopted an ecological approach, grouping specimens of animals and plants from particular habitats together, and labelling them to explain something of their ecological interrelationships (ill. 24). Such exhibitions are more broadly informative than the traditional ones were, and exploit the resources of modern graphic art to increase the impact on the visitor. Labels are in general longer than they used to be, use colour and varied type faces, and frequently incorporate drawings, maps and photographs.

A still more recent development is to adopt an approach which is frankly and openly even more didactic. The museum gallery is seen as a medium for teaching the fundamental scientific concepts of biology. Thus an ecology exhibit could concentrate on an abstract

# A BEECHWOOD IN OCTOBER

24. Natural history gallery display, Buckinghamshire County Museum, Aylesbury

principle such as the flow of energy in an ecosystem (ill. 25) rather than on a taxonomic treatment of the organisms present in the habitat; or, instead of exhibiting a range of specimens in which may be discerned more or less incidentally the adaptations of animals and plants to the environment, the idea of adaptation could be taken as the theme of a particular display.

Besides these approaches, the concepts that lie behind the outward appearances of natural history specimens, such as those that have become established in the field of molecular biology, could be taken as a starting point. This abstract approach requires more explanation than was thought necessary in old fashioned museum exhibitions and, where possible, all the technical innovations of modern audiovisual presentation are called upon. The only limit to

25. The 'Introducing Ecology' exhibition at the British Museum (Natural History). This section of it is concerned with energy flow through ecosystems

their employment is cost, both of the initial construction and the day-to-day maintenance.

**Educational services**
Increasingly, museums of all kinds are employing professional staff with a purely interpretative function in addition to curators, researchers and display designers. Sometimes the local education committee seconds a teacher to the museum for this purpose, but in the larger institutions there is a permanent full-time education officer with one or more assistants. The employment of part-time volunteers, which is widespread in natural history museums in America where they are usually termed 'docents' is not yet common in Britain, although the Education Section of the British Museum

(Natural History) trains and employs a team of volunteer auxiliaries to help with its interpretative work with school children.

Inevitably education officers devote much of their time to school parties, but they are also interested in assisting individuals, both young people and adults. Frequently courses of lectures are given, often in collaboration with local adult education services or university extension departments, which are of great interest and value to the amateur.

The education officer is also the best person to approach in the first instance with natural history enquiries or when help is needed to identify a specimen. He will know the capabilities and limitations of his particular institution, and be able to advise accordingly. Often he can provide the answer to a general enquiry at once; with more detailed questions, he can usually direct enquirers to the relevant reference books, and if necessary refer them to the curator of the appropriate collection.

## Co-operation with amateurs

What amateur naturalists can learn from the displays in the galleries clearly depends on the museum. In some of the larger ones they may be able to improve their understanding of scientific principles and perhaps deepen their insight into such applications in the natural world. In many, both large and small, they may find something new on the subject of ecological studies. In some small ones the emphasis may be local, and they can learn what to look for in what may be to them an unfamiliar part of the country. In others it must be admitted all they may find out is which foreign parts were visited by the local worthies who donated or bequeathed their collections. The help that amateur naturalists can offer to the museum in connection with its public displays will vary similarly: the large museums with permanent teams of designers will not be able to make use of them; but in the small museums, which are usually chronically understaffed, they may be very welcome.

## Reserve collections

The main concern of amateur naturalists, however, is likely to be behind the scenes. They will wish to familiarize themselves with the appearance of a range of natural history specimens with a view to being able to recognize them in the field, and so they will turn to the reserve collections. Again, the amount of help they will get and can offer will vary widely from museum to museum.

There are in Britain several major museums of international importance (see section on Locating useful collections p. 105). All these employ scientific staff who are engaged in research on the collections, so that expert advice is available as well as specimens and the relevant books and journals in the accompanying specialist libraries. Local museums, even when they possess useful collections, may be unable to employ anyone to work on them at all. In such cases knowledgeable amateurs may be able to offer valuable help. Assistance with routine curatorial work that is outside the scope of ordinary clerical staff is often required. The work that needs doing may range from remounting pressed plants and repacketing other specimens to checking labels and identifications and perhaps updating nomenclature.

The donation of specimens to fill gaps in collections is something the amateur can often do, and it is welcomed by both large and small museums.

## Museums and conservation

As with opinions about the general functions of museums and the types of audience to which they should appeal, attitudes to collecting have changed in this century. One hundred years ago an interest in natural history was regarded as almost synonymous with collecting specimens; now it is generally considered to be perfectly possible to make progress in the study of the subject without making a collection in the old sense at all.

Naturalists, both professional and amateur, are now inclined to direct much of their field activity to collecting records (see Chapter 4). The motivation behind this is largely a widely held and profound conviction of the importance of wildlife conservation, but the new role of local museums as record centres, which is discussed later in this chapter, is another incentive.

The change of approach has been made possible by improved techniques. Accurate identifications can often be made in the field now that an extensive literature for this purpose is available. In particular the proliferation of workable keys to many groups of organisms, largely brought about by research on museum collections, has made an important contribution. The comparative simplicity of obtaining clear and detailed photographs with modern films and cameras makes possible the collection of accurate and permanent records without gathering accompanying specimens.

Nevertheless, it may be necessary to take some specimens for further examination, especially those in difficult groups, although it is usual nowadays to do so only on a very limited scale. In any case, before embarking upon the collection of natural history specimens of any sort, it is essential to ascertain the legal position, which is now much more restrictive than it used to be (see Chapter 9).

Changes in the law and in public attitudes make the collections that already exist in our museums all the more precious, as much of them is irreplaceable. All field naturalists who make limited specialized collections in the course of their studies should seriously consider donating them to a museum when they have finished active work with the specimens.

**Data banks** (see also chapter 4)
Most amateurs seem to enjoy making lists of species they have observed and identified, primarily for their own interest; but if such records are compiled in a systematic way they can be of use to others as well. Precise indications of location are essential. This is a simple matter now that the National Grid appears on the majority of maps amateurs are likely to use, not only on all those produced by the Ordnance Survey but also on those published by such organizations as the Automobile Association.

Notes on the nature of the habitat should also be made. In fact, the most useful lists are as complete as possible for a particular group in a clearly defined and characterized area. Museums are increasingly becoming involved in storing records of this kind, and the national and county museums have embarked upon installing what have come to be termed 'data banks'. In their simplest form, data banks are card indexes, but computer techniques are increasingly used.

The establishment and functioning of these record stores is co-ordinated by the Biological Records Centre at Monks Wood Experimental Station, Abbots Ripton. The corresponding organization for the Republic of Ireland is at St Martins House, Waterloo Road, Dublin. Regional Biological Record Centres have been established for Scotland at the Museum, Dundee, for Northern Ireland at the Ulster Museum, Belfast, and for Wales at the National Museum of Wales, Cardiff. Most English counties have their own Regional Biological Record Centres, usually based on the county museum.

Amateur naturalists can make valuable contributions to the record stores; even small numbers of records and incomplete lists, provided they are accurate, are required for most groups of organisms. Of course, as with the other functions of museums, the ideal relationship between museum and amateur in this connection is two-way, and the record centres are sources of information as well as recipients of it.

## Instructions for collectors

Since the turn of the century the British Museum (Natural History) has produced a series of publications under the general title of *Instructions to Collectors*. These vary in scope and detail from quite brief pamphlets to more substantial booklets which contain various items of information useful to the amateur naturalist. No. 10 *Plants* (72 pp.) contains full instructions for pressing and drying plant specimens, and includes notes on special techniques for particular groups such as aquatic plants, algae, fungi and lichens. The section on palms is of limited value in Britain, but the sensible advice about labels and the date that should accompany each specimen are of universal application.

No. 4 *Insects* (169 pp.) has an introductory section on classification (ill. 26) and the position of the Insecta within the Arthropoda, the development and life history of insects, and some other matters such as zoogeography. Methods of trapping, mounting and preserving are dealt with very fully; there is an appendix of useful recipes, and three pages of bibliography. Half the book is devoted to a useful and well illustrated outline classification of insects.

No. 1 *Mammals* (55 pp.) gives a full account of the various methods of trapping mammals, including notes on what might be called 'inadvertent' methods, such as looking for mammalian

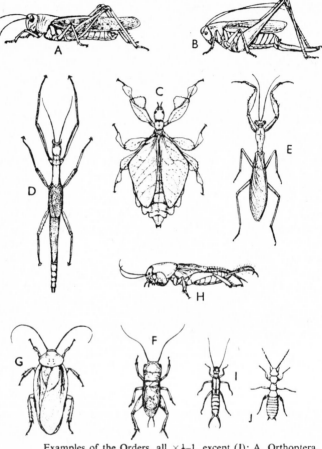

Examples of the Orders, all ×½–1, except (J): A, Orthoptera, Acrididae—a locust; B, Orthoptera, Tetrigidae—a grouse-locust; C, Phasmida—a leaf-insect; D, Phasmida—a stick-insect; E, Dictyoptera, Mantidae—a praying mantis; F, Orthoptera, Gryllidae—a cricket; G, Dictyoptera, Blattidae—a cockroach; H, Orthoptera, Gryllotalpidae—a mole-cricket; I, Dermaptera—an earwig; J, Zoraptera—*Zorotypus* (×8).

26. An illustration from the fifth (revised) edition of *Instructions for collectors, No. 4a: Insects*, published by the British Museum (Natural History)

remains in discarded bottles in which small creatures frequently become caught and are unable to escape. The most useful section is that describing the method of mounting skins of small animals, including bats, on card.

No. 2 *Birds* (48 pp.) and the other *Instructions* listed in table 3, p. 108, are, on the other hand, intended more exclusively for the professional collector operating abroad, and are of little interest in the context of this book.

## Locating useful collections

Collections of natural history specimens of interest to amateurs are to be found in the galleries of the great national museums and of local museums both large and small. The amount of material on direct public view varies of course from museum to museum, not only with the policies of the curators but also with the group of organisms involved. Plant specimens are usually mainly in reserve collections referred to as herbaria, and insects also are more often than not housed behind the scenes. Vertebrate specimens and fossil material on the other hand lend themselves more readily to public display and often form the major part of the public exhibition. The amateur will wish to gain access to the collections in reserve as well as those in the galleries. Individuals would be well advised, however, to become familiar with the contents of the local museum before proceeding to consult others further afield, and in general to leave the major collections until last.

The general natural history collections in the British Museum (Natural History) are of major importance. General collections of great regional importance are housed in the Royal Scottish Museum in Edinburgh, the National Museum of Wales in Cardiff and the National Museum of Ireland in Dublin. Other major collections are: plants in the Herbarium of the Royal Botanic Gardens, Kew: vertebrates generally in the Oxford University Museum and the Cambridge University Museum of Zoology; birds in particular at the Zoological Museum, Tring; insects in the Hope Department of Entomology, Oxford; and fossils in the Sedgewick Museum, Cambridge and the Hunterian Museum, Glasgow.

More information is available on herbaria than on other kinds of collections, and McNeill (1968) discusses their role in botanical

studies and lists amongst others the University Natural History
Museum, Aberdeen, the City Museum, Birmingham, the Merseyside
Museums, Liverpool, the University Museum, Manchester, and the
Museum, Leicester, as containing important regional herbaria in
addition to those mentioned above. *British herbaria* by Kent (1958)
is a useful work of reference containing basic information about
more than 200 herbaria. About 160 of these are housed in local
museums, although McNeill estimated that not more than about
twenty of them were active, working herbaria. He mentions the
Royal Albert Museum, Exeter, as an example of a large and active
local herbarium.

Unfortunately for other groups there is no work of comparable
scope. In 1940 C. D. Sherborn published a useful and amusing book
entitled *Where is the —— Collection?* The sub-title 'an account of
the various natural history collections which have come to the notice
of the compiler' gives a good idea of the contents. Museums are not
listed, but rather collectors, and the present localities of their
collections are given. He also includes other snippets of information
about individuals, some of it rather scurrilous.

For insects, there is a somewhat similar but much more extensive
work by Horn and Kahle entitled *Über entomologische Sammlungen*
which appeared between 1935 and 1937; this work is unfortunately
difficult to come by.

For fossils, Woodward and Sherborn mention in the introduction
to *A catalogue of British fossil vertebrata* (1890) the locations of the
main nineteenth century collections. These last works are not
gazetteers of museums, but lists of collections under the names of the
collectors. To find out what is in a particular museum there is no
substitute for local enquiry, either at the local museum or the
regional Biological Records Centre (see page 84).

## How to make use of a natural history museum

It is a good idea to begin by gaining a general impression of what is
on display in the public galleries. Most museums have some sort of
a bookstall or bookshop whose stock includes a guide to the
museum. Some museums provide general guided tours of the
galleries; these are usually interesting and informative, but amateur
naturalists with a serious purpose will probably wish to avoid them.

When an impression of the museum has been formed, questions may be directed in the first place to the education officer who is probably in the best position to appreciate the nature of the resources. In very small museums the director, curator and education officer are often one and the same person.

Some thought must be given to the questions to be asked, and the best advice on this important point is to make them as specific as possible. The answers to very general questions, such as those that are often set as projects for school children, are better pursued amongst the shelves of natural history books at a public library or within the pages of an encyclopaedia.

If a natural history specimen requires identification, make sure that it is worth the trouble that might be involved. It should be an adequate specimen, and it should be in a reasonable state of preservation. It is only reasonable, too, that the enquirer should make every effort to name the specimen to the best of his knowledge and ability. It is better to say 'I think this is a carabid beetle; will you please tell me which one?', than 'Can you tell me what insect this is?'; or, 'Will you tell me which species of *Cladonia* this is?' rather than 'What is this lichen?'.

These considerations apply with even greater force when writing to the museum rather than making a personal call; in addition, the enquirer should enclose a gummed label with his name and address and stamps to cover return postage (this is better than a stamped addressed envelope, as the one supplied may not be the right size if the museum returns a reading list or other leaflet with the answer to the query). Specimens sent for identification should be good ones, properly preserved and carefully packed.

As far as possible, make the relationship with the museum two-way; present any interesting specimens if the curator says he would like to have them, and make field records available for the files.

### References and further reading

Alexander, E. 1974. *Museums and how to use them*. London: Batsford.

Anon. 1978. *Nature at work: Introducing ecology*. London: British Museum (Natural History).

Anon. 1979. *Museums and galleries in Great Britain and Ireland*. Dunstable: ABC Publications.

Horn, W. & Kahle, I. 1935–37. Uber entomologische Sammlungen. *Entomologische Beihefte aus Berlin–Dahlun*, Band 2–4.

Hudson, K. & Nicholls, A. 1975. *Directory of museums.* London: Macmillan.

Kent, D. H. 1958. *British herbaria.* London: Botanical Society of the British Isles.

McNeill, J. 1968. Regional and local herbaria. In *Modern methods in plant taxonomy* (ed. V. H. Heywood): 33–44. London: Academic Press.

Sherborn, C. D. 1940. *Where is the —— collection?* Cambridge: Cambridge University Press.

Woodward, A. S. & Sherborn, C. D. 1890. *A catalogue of British fossil vertebrata.* London: British Museum (Natural History).

TABLE 3

Instructions for collectors published by the British Museum (Natural History).

| No. | Date of first edition | Current edition |
|-----|-----------------------|-----------------|
| 1 | 1900 | *Mammals*, 6th edn, 1968 |
| 2 | 1900 | *Birds*, 1st edn of new series, 1970 (10th edn) |
| 3 | 1891 | *Reptiles, batrachians and fishes*, 6th edn 1953 superseded by *Fishes*, 1st edn, 1965 |
| 4 | 1899 | *Insects*, 5th edn of new series, 1974 (13th edn) |
| 5 | 1900 | *Diptera*, 4th edn, 1919 |
| 6 | 1898 | *Mosquitoes*, 4th edn, 1919 |
| 7 | 1904 | *Blood sucking flies, ticks, etc.*, 5th edn, 1926 |
| 8 | 1900 | *Spiders, centipedes, etc.*, 4th edn, 1924 |
| 9 | 1900 | *Invertebrates other than insects*, 2nd edn of new series, 1954 (6th edn) |
| 10 | 1900 | *Plants*, 6th edn, 1957 |
| 11 | 1900 | *Fossils and Minerals*, 9th edn, 1970 |
| 12 | 1916 | *Worms*, 2nd edn, 1938 |

# 7. Zoos and wildlife parks

John Stidworthy

Zoos have much to offer the naturalist. In them are gathered animals from all over the world, which otherwise could only be seen with much expensive travel, and perhaps even then with difficulty. For many people they are simply places to take the children, but adults can appreciate more than children the recreation and information available from an animal collection. For many kinds of animal this is the only chance there is of appreciating their real size, comportment and nature, hearing their characteristic sounds and savouring their characteristic smells. This is true not only for exotic animals but for some British ones. There must be many keen naturalists who have never seen an otter or a wild-cat alive except in a zoo or wildlife park.

For many animals little is known, or will ever be known, about the details of their normal behaviour in the wild, and therefore zoo and wildlife park observations can prove very valuable. Some zoologists argue that captivity disrupts normal behaviour, but in most cases, particularly in the more up-to-date zoos, there seems little evidence of pathological behaviour. Much has been discovered about behaviour and communication simply by watching animals in zoos, as at Chester Zoo for example. Another useful aspect of zoos is that they may be able to provide speedy comparisons with related species, without having to venture too far.

Many of the larger old-established zoos have very wide interests, but some of the newer zoos and parks specialize in animals of particular groups. Thus anyone with an interest in monkeys and apes should visit Twycross for the sake of the primate collection there and Paignton too if they can: both these zoos also have reptile collections worth a visit. At Marwell the main emphasis of the collection is on hoofed animals (ill. 27) and carnivores. British and European animals are a speciality of the Norfolk Wildlife Park; Kilverstone Wildlife Park concentrates on animals from the New World.

Some people feel that safari parks provide a kinder alternative to the traditional zoo. This is probably not the case, and just as there are traditional zoos with high standards and humane husbandry of

27. The important conservation function of zoos is illustrated by the Scimitar-horned Oryx, which breeds successfully at Marwell Zoological Park near Winchester

animals and some which are not so good, so it is with safari parks. It is probably a mistake to assume that they are more natural than zoos and, of course, only a limited range of animals are suitable for the safari park treatment.

It is anthropomorphism to suggest that all animals need large cages. Some do, and some will use them, but for many animals space is not, beyond the needs of reasonable exercise and territory formation, a prime consideration. A small cage which caters imaginatively for the animals' needs, whether they be for climbing, burrowing, swimming, privacy or any other factor, may be far better than several acres used with less imagination. Another disadvantage of safari parks for studying animals is that the observer himself is much restricted, and, at peak times, not really able to loiter.

The *raison d'être* of zoos can be summed up in four words: research, education, conservation and entertainment.

The research function of zoos is largely invisible to the general public. The leader in this field in Britain is the Zoological Society of London, and the results of the studies carried out there are communicated through scientific journals, and in publications dealing specifically with animals in captivity. Articles of many kinds concerning wild animal husbandry appear in the *International Zoo Year Book*. Information is passed between keepers via the *Journal of the Association of British Wild Animal Keepers*.

Most zoos claim to be educational and indeed some zoos employ education officers. The London Zoo was one of the pioneers, and now employs four graduates to give talks and tours to parties of school children ranging in age from seven to eighteen. Each year some 60 000 pupils make use of these facilities. Paignton Zoo also has been active in this field for a long time. Newer education schemes are in operation at Edinburgh and Glasgow, and some of the smaller zoos are also taking on an active educational role.

Some zoos, free of the pressure of numbers which forces London Zoo to concentrate on school parties, are able to provide a range of services to include the general adult public and individual child visitors. Another feature of the educational activities is the running of children's clubs, whose aim may be to teach the children some zoology, to involve them with the life of the zoo, or both.

Contrary to much popular belief, no zoo or wildlife park in Britain is run or supported financially from Government sources, and Britain is unusual in that no major zoo is a municipal undertaking—with the exception of the relatively new Blackpool Zoological Gardens of which much may be expected in the future. Most of the major zoos in Britain are owned by societies; these provide privileges in the form of free admission for their members, and often free or reduced admission for their guests. For those interested in animals, membership of the local or national society is well worth while. Some privately owned zoos also run societies; Marwell Zoological Park, for example, offers free admission and regular bulletins for members of its society.

Conservation is becoming an ever greater concern of zoos, and some now consider their most important functions to be teaching about the need for conservation, and the keeping, particularly the breeding, of rare and endangered species. There are many aspects to the conservation problem, and zoos have sometimes enjoyed a less than happy relationship with some sections of the conservation lobby and animal welfare societies. That there should be any great degree of conflict is a pity, for most conservationists and reputable zoos are really on the same side. Of course any naturalist must have mixed feelings about any proposal to bring into captivity wild individuals from a threatened population, but this may be the best way of trying to save a species. Without captive breeding programmes the world would by now have lost the Père David's deer, the European bison, the Hawaiian goose, and probably Przewalski's horse (ill. 28). There are animal species for which the future looks increasingly bleak and it is perhaps better to bring a few individuals into captivity now and discover the regime under which they will thrive and breed before it is too late.

The breeding of rare animals in zoos and wildlife parks is a contribution though not a solution to conservation. There are still some animals which zoos have not succeeded in breeding; and there simply may not be the room in zoos for all endangered animals. The answer, of course, is to return these animals where possible to the wild, but often it is precisely because they are not safe there that they are being bred in captivity. Ideally attention should be

28. Part of the herd of Przewalski horses at Marwell Zoological Park. Here these ancestors of our domesticated horses can be observed under almost natural conditions

primarily focused on conserving the natural habitats of rare and endangered species. It is distressing that even certain British species can readily be seen only in captivity. It may have to be accepted that although zoos may be a vital last resort for rare animals, their main use is to acquaint people with the need for conservation and allow them to see, if possible, the species for which they should feel concern.

Another type of conservation to which an increasing amount of attention is being paid is the preservation of the rarer breeds of farm animals. The arguments for the retention of viable numbers of these breeds include aesthetic considerations, scientific interest in their genetics and the effects and processes of domestication, and the more utilitarian agricultural considerations of keeping breeding stocks with genetic characteristics that may be useful in the future even if they are not valued today.

Activity in this field has now largely passed from traditional zoos and wildlife parks to interested individuals and farmers, and to farm parks—the domestic equivalent of zoos—of which the largest and best known is the Cotswold Park at Guiting Power, Gloucestershire. Important breeding centres recognized by the Rare Breeds Survival Trust display the Chartley bull's head symbol of the Trust. There are also many zoos which still display one or more of the interesting domestic breeds such as Jacob's sheep or Chartley cattle, and one zoo, Drusilla's in Sussex, is a recognized breeding centre.

**Some zoo societies**

Bristol, Clifton and West of England Zoological Society, Clifton, Bristol BS8 3HA

Jersey Wildlife Preservation Trust, Les Augres Manor, Jersey

Marwell Zoological Society, Marwell Zoological Park, Colden Common, Winchester, Hants SO21 1JH

North of England Zoological Society, Zoological Gardens, Upton-by-Chester, Cheshire CH2 1LH

Peacock Association, Herbert Whitley Trust, Paignton Zoological Gardens, Torbay, Devon TQ4 5JS

The Pheasant Trust, Great Witchingham, Norwich NOR 65X

The Rare Breeds Survival Trust, Winkleigh, Devon EX19 8SQ

The Royal Zoological Society of Scotland, Scottish National Zoological Park, Murrayfield, Edinburgh EH12 6TS

The Wildfowl Trust, New Grounds, Slimbridge, Glos. GL2 7BT
The Zoological Society of Glasgow and West of Scotland,
    Calderpark, Uddingston, Glasgow G71 7RZ
The Zoological Society of London, Regent's Park, London
    NW1 4RY
Other British zoos and aquaria are listed in: Olney, P. J. S. (ed.)
    1978. *International Zoo Year Book*, no. 18. London: Zoological
    Society.

## Further reading

Bergamar, K. 1969. *Zoos, bird gardens and animal collections in
    Great Britain and Eire*. Tring: Shire Publications.
Chinery, M. 1976. *Life in the zoo*. London: Collins.
Fisher, J. 1966. *Zoos of the world*. London: Aldus Books.
Fitter, R. S. R. & Scott, P. 1978. *The penitent butchers*. London:
    Collins and Fauna Preservation Society.
Hatley, J. 1972. *The Observer's book of zoo animals*. London:
    Warne.
Hediger, H. 1955. *Psychology of animals in zoos*. London:
    Butterworths.
Hediger, H. 1970. *Man and animal in the zoo*. London: Routledge &
    Kegan Paul.
Robins, K. & Radford, M. 1974–6. *Guide to zoos, zoological gardens
    and bird gardens in the British Isles*. Burnham: Inter-Zoo
    Publications.
Schomberg, G. 1970. *The Penguin guide to British zoos*.
    Harmondsworth: Penguin Books.
Smith, A. 1977. *Animals on view*. London: Weidenfeld & Nicolson.
Stanbury, P. 1972. *Looking at mammals*. London: Heinemann
    Educational.
Williamson, K. & Schomberg, G. 1976. *Wildlife in Britain*.
    Basingstoke: Automobile Association.
Zuckerman, S. *et al.*, (eds.) 1976. *The Zoological Society of London
    1826–1976 and beyond*. (Zoological Society Symposium no. 40)
    London: Academic Press.

## Periodicals

*The Ark* (The Rare Breeds Survival Trust, The Ark, Winkleigh,
    Devon EX19 8SQ.)

*The International Zoo Year Book* (The Zoological Society of London, Regent's Park, London NW1 4RY.)

*Wildlife* (Wildlife Publications Ltd., Berkeley Square House, 14 Berkeley Square, London W1X 5PB.)

*Zoo Federation News* (The Federation of Zoos, Zoological Gardens, Regent's Park, London NW1 4RY.)

# 8. Nature trails

Susan M. Joy and John Stidworthy

Before National Nature Week in 1963, nature trails were almost unknown in Britain, but their value as an educational tool was recognized so quickly that today they are to be found extensively throughout the countryside and increasingly in towns and cities. Essentially a nature trail is a signposted walk devised to introduce the visitor to the animals and plants and other interesting features in a locality, enabling many people to find greater enjoyment in Britain's wildlife and to reach a better understanding of the need for nature conservation. (ill. 29.)

Self-guiding nature trails are of two types: those where display boards or labels are provided along the pathway or those where simple numbered posts at points of interest on the ground are used in conjunction with an explanatory leaflet. The features illustrated may be geographical, ecological, botanical or zoological. Sometimes instead of numbered points there is just an explanatory map of the trail in the leaflet indicating the main viewpoints; this has been done for the trail at Tring Reservoirs National Nature Reserve in Hertfordshire. However, in places which to the layman have fewer obvious features, such as woodland or moor, such a method may be less useful.

It is important to note that the information imparted at each point of interest is a guide to the background and changing pattern of life of a natural community and not a detailed catalogue of what might be seen. Although trails are usually designed to ensure that they include something of interest all the year round, many of the things described can only be seen at certain seasons. In winter, for example, birds are observed to the best advantage, but in summer flowers and insects are more conspicuous. Equally the time of day will also affect the things to be seen; in early morning birds will be more frequent than on a summer's afternoon with many people about, and dusk is certainly a better time for observing most mammals. For this reason nature trails often indicate places where traces of animal occupation such as tracks, food remains, droppings or nests may be found.

The nature trail at the National Trust Ashridge Estate in

Hertfordshire for example, points out places where deer tracks may be found and describes their appearance; it indicates where hazel nuts are left by woodmice after gnawing and when there are marks left by woodcock; and it also lists some of the commoner invertebrate species which may be found feeding on particular clumps of plants.

For a competent naturalist a nature trail in a familiar area may be unnecessary but for many beginners it can be very helpful; even an experienced naturalist visiting an unfamiliar area might gain valuable knowledge of it from a nature trail.

A useful type of nature trail which poses questions and provides a selection of answers for the visitor has recently been developed at Losehill Hall, the Peak National Park Study Centre. This trail guide includes a minimum of information with a format designed to be the starting point for discussion of conservation issues with the aim of

29. A nature trail becomes all the more interesting if visitors can be accompanied by an expert. A woodland walk for novices is here led by the well-known ornithologist, Dr Bruce Campbell.

involving the public not merely in the facts and figures but also in the whys and wherefores. For example, a description is given of a small stream that runs along the edge of the parkland which rises on the shale ridge behind Losehill Hall and its appearance and use. The following question is then posed:

'The stream is an additional area of wildlife habitat within the Hall grounds. Would you,
(a)   Leave it as it is?
(b)   Create a truly marshy area by ponding part of the stream and fence it off from the grazing land?
(c)   Sacrifice the view and plant alders and willow trees along the banks as shelter and food for the birds?'

and later where a bird watching hide is provided:

'If more birds could be attracted to the vicinity of the bird hide, visitors would be sure of a good show when they spend an hour or two in the hide. In order to do this, would you,
(a)   Put up more nest boxes?
(b)   Provide visitors with packets of bird seeds?
(c)   Plant native berrying bushes nearby, to increase the natural food supply?'

Certainly this is a nature trail with a difference and it is undoubtedly an interesting and effective method of helping visitors to understand the natural history, wildlife and landscape conservation of an area.

As at Losehill Hall, a nature trail is very often part of a complex of facilities provided for the site and used in conjunction with interpretative centres. At Witley Common, Surrey, for example, exhibits, photographs and filmshows in the centre provide the background information to the locality, while the trails extend the learning experience to the field. Here several alternative nature trails of varying length are provided. Each trail is distinguished by differently coloured way markers; the red trail leads through woodland and heathland habitats; the blue trail introduces the visitor to man-made habitats; while the orange trail passes through an old army camp site which has attracted a large variety of birds.

Variation in distance and route of trails caters for all age ranges, walking abilities and interests. Generally speaking $\frac{1}{2}$ km is the minimum distance and 5 km the maximum distance for a trail.

A more specialized and comprehensive type of nature trail, designed to interest the naturalist and student rather than the casual visitor, is illustrated by the trail at Tregaron Bog in Wales. Leased by the Nature Conservancy Council and designated as a National Nature Reserve, Tregaron Bog consists of valley bog vegetation with extensive beds of *Juncus* (rushes) and *Eriophorum* (cotton sedges). Within the area there are also three raised bogs which have developed as a result of water-logged conditions with a consequent build up of peat into dome shaped areas. The south east raised bog has a nature trail which provides an introduction to the plant associations that can be found there; a guide gives a detailed description of what can be seen.

Among the many organizations now providing nature trails are the Nature Conservancy Council, the National Trust, the Field Studies Council, the Royal Society for the Protection of Birds, the Forestry Commission, the Nature Conservation Trusts, and even bodies such as the Central Electricity Generating Board. Other trails are run by local natural history societies, private groups, or by local authorities through their museum or park departments. A booklet detailing many of the nature trails open to the general public in the United Kingdom is available, when in print, from the British Tourist Authority, 64 St James's Street, London SW1A 1NF. Although the list contains hundreds of examples with map references, distance and type of trail, cost and means of access, it is by no means exhaustive and those intent on finding trails should also make enquiries of local naturalists, museums, natural history societies and tourist offices, which may have details of those not nationally publicized. The National Trust, 42 Queen Anne's Gate, London SW1H 9AS also publish a list of eighty five trails on their properties in England, Wales and Northern Ireland; copies are free on receipt of a large stamped addressed envelope.

**Provisions for the handicapped**
In addition to the provision of nature trails for active naturalists there is a growing awareness of the need to make the countryside

enjoyable and accessible for the disabled wherever possible. The Trent Park Nature Trail, managed by the Greater London Parks Department, is one of many trails that have been designed for the visually handicapped. Special pathways have been constructed and marked out to guide blind visitors safely along the trail, and features of interest are described by Braille labels mounted on posts. A similar but more comprehensive trail has recently been provided at the Wildfowl Trust's Reserve at Slimbridge. Parties of visually handicapped visitors that book in advance are given an introductory talk by a member of the Trust's staff who uses an exhibition of stuffed birds, wings, etc. to give an idea of size, texture and shape of different groups of wildfowl. A relief map of the grounds, made of materials of different textures, is also available so that visitors can orientate themselves before walking around the grounds. A pre-recorded commentary about each stopping point and the birds that can be heard calling there is given to each individual for their walk around the nature trail. Individuals in small escorted groups that have not booked can, for a small charge, hire a player and cassette.

A special guide to nature trails *An Access Guide to the Nature Reserves of England, Scotland and Wales for the Disabled* (price 20p) available from the Royal Association for Disablement and Rehabilitation, 25 Mortimer Street, London W1N 8AB has been prepared by a member of the RSPB staff. It lists all the reserves that a disabled person in a wheelchair or with a walking difficulty can visit in comfort; there are fifty seven of them, ranging from Aberdeenshire to Anglesey to Suffolk. The emphasis is on bird-watching, as this is the easiest wildlife study to do from a wheelchair.

## Town and farm trails

Nature trails have been extended into towns and cities and on to farms, and may even be undertaken by car. Town trails may combine a wide range of natural features with elements of local history and from them much may be discovered about the wildlife of urban areas, whose existence few people realize. Geological trails, such as the one prepared by the Geological Museum on building stones to be seen in London, can also be successful in urban areas. The establishment of farm trails has led to an increasing concern for reconciling farming activities with wildlife interests and just as important these trails help the public, naturalist and layman, to understand the working of the farm. These two elements have been successfully combined at the Norton Farm Trail in Sussex where the factors involved in running a modern farm enterprise are considered with regard to the landscape and wildlife conservation interests (illus. 30 and 31). At the Trent Park Farm Trail, four seasonal guides give naturalists an opportunity to discover the temporal changes which take place in the wildlife throughout the farming year.

## Natural trails as management tools

One of the primary advantages of nature trails to the recreational planner has been as a management tool in areas which are heavily visited and used by the public. Sometimes it is very important for the wildlife of such areas that numbers of visitors are kept low or carefully regulated; trails can channel people into those parts which are the least sensitive to human disturbance, so that damage to rare species or delicate habitats is avoided. At the same time people are informed about wildlife and this can only benefit the study of natural history and wildlife conservation in the long term.

## Further reading

Binks, G. 1978. *Self-guided trails: an appraisal of 46 self guided trails* prepared by the Dartington Amenity Research Trust, for the British Tourist Authority, British Waterways Board, Countryside Commission, Department of the Environment, Forestry Commission and Nature Conservancy Council. Cheltenham: Countryside Commission.

Countryside Commission 1979. *Recreation for the Disabled.* Bibliography No. 3. Cheltenham: Countryside Commission.

Goodey, B. 1974. *Urban Walks and Town Trails.* Birmingham University: Centre for Urban and Regional Studies.

Spray, M. 1975. Trails: an alternative to the field demonstration. *Journal of Biological Education* **9**, 209–213.

Wray, E. V. 1968. Nature trails as a teaching aid. *Journal of Biological Education* **2**, 21–38.

30. A nature trail can help interpret features of the landscape as well as draw attention to interesting plants and animals. Here three boys from an Inner London Youth Club have their eyes opened to the wildlife and scenery of Dorset.

31. A map of Norton's Farm Trail

## Nature trail guides

*Nature trails in Britain* (when in print) is available from the British
   Tourist Authority, 64 St James's Street, London SW1A 1NF.
*Nature walks* is available from the National Trust, 42 Queen Anne's
   Gate, London SW1H 9AS, on receipt of a large stamped
   addressed envelope.

## Nature trails to visit

Beinn Eighe National Reserve Trail, Kinlochewe, Wester Ross,
   Scotland.
Bolderwood Walks, New Forest, Lyndhurst, Hampshire.
Butser Trail, Queen Elizabeth Country Park, Gravel Hill,
   Horndean, Near Portsmouth.
Gower Coast National Nature Reserve Limestone Nature Trail,
   Rhossili, Gower, West Glamorgan, South Wales.
Inverpolly National Nature Reserve Trail, Near Elphin, Wester
   Ross, Scotland.
Langley Park Nature Trail, Near Slough, Buckinghamshire.
Losehill Hall Nature Trail, Castleton, Derbyshire.
Norton Farm Nature Trail, Sedlescombe, Near Hastings, East
   Sussex.
Plackett Walk, Abbot's Wood, Bedgebury (Friston) Forest.
Rivelin Nature Trail, Rivelin Valley, Sheffield.
Roddlesworth Nature Trail, Tockholes, Near Darwen, Lancashire.
Trent Park Nature Trail for the Blind, Barnet, Hertfordshire.
Trent Park Farm Trail, Barnet, Hertfordshire.
Tring Reservoir National Nature Reserve Trail, Tring,
   Hertfordshire.
Witley Common Nature Trail, Milford, Near Guildford, Surrey.
Wye and Crundale National Nature Reserve, Wye, Near Ashford,
   Kent.

# 9. Wildlife and the law

Tim S. Sands

The widespread interest in Britain in conserving our wildlife and those places in which it can live successfully has coincided with, and been prompted by, the growing pressures on our countryside. It is this basic appreciation of the value of the natural world by the public which has provided the climate within which Parliament has recently passed new laws against those persons who would wilfully kill or destroy endangered or harmless animals and plants. Generally, however, legislative safeguards for wildlife have been developed in a rather *ad hoc* fashion and do not accord with one general principle or philosophy.

This chapter summarizes under three headings those laws which are of special concern to naturalists: (1) protection of endangered or vulnerable species; (2) conservation of areas of scientific interest; and (3) more general provisions. Although some laws apply to the whole of the United Kingdom it should not be assumed that all English and Welsh law applies to Scotland. The law in Northern Ireland also differs on many points.

## 1. Protection of endangered or vulnerable species

The law that applies specifically to species protection is confined in relation to endangered species, to parts of the **Protection of Birds Act 1954–67** as amended, the major part of the **Conservation of Wild Creatures and Wild Plants Act 1975**, and the **Endangered Species (Import and Export) Act 1976**. The law in relation to species which are hunted for sport or for their commercial value or as pests is contained in the **Conservation of Seals Act 1970**, the **Deer Acts 1959** and **1963**, parts of the **Protection of Birds Act 1954–67** as amended, and to the **Badgers Act 1973**. This chapter does not cover the regulations on the import and export of wild animals and plants. Licences are required for such trade in most cases and enquiries should be made to both the Ministry of Agriculture, Fisheries and Food and the Department of the Environment if there is any doubt as to the regulations.

For convenience it seems preferable to discuss all bird legislation together. Although there are some exceptions, the basic principle of the **Protection of Birds Act** 1954–67 is that all wild birds and their nests and eggs are protected by law. The 1954 Act repealed several acts passed from 1869 onwards. The Sea Birds and Preservation Act protecting the seabirds on the Yorkshire coast cliffs at Flamborough and Dempton had been passed in 1869; 11 years later, in 1880, the first fairly comprehensive Bird Act was passed.

The law as it stands today makes it an offence 'wilfully to kill, injure or take, or attempt to kill, injure or take any wild bird, to take, damage or destroy its nest; take or destroy a wild bird's egg; ring or mark any wild bird; or have in one's possession or control any wild bird recently killed or taken which cannot be proved to have been killed or taken legally'.

There are many exceptions to these general rules: for instance, the taking of a wild bird that has been injured other than by an individual's own actions with the aim of caring for it and releasing it later is not an offence; and a person may be granted a licence by the Department of the Environment, the Nature Conservancy Council (NCC) and the Ministry of Agriculture, Fisheries and Food to permit an otherwise prohibited act—for example, the taking of certain birds for ringing or marking. In addition, certain 'pest' species may be killed or taken by authorized persons provided they use legitimate means and these are listed in Schedule 2 to the Act. Recognized quarry species which may be killed or taken by legitimate means, outside their close season, appear in Schedule 3 to the Act.

The normal maximum penalty for an offence under the Act is a fine of £50 per bird, nest, egg or skin; however, anyone found guilty of an offence punishable by a special penalty, for example, the killing or taking of the country's rarest species—listed in Schedule 1 to the Act—or the use of prohibited methods, is now liable to a fine of up to £500. Wilful disturbance of a first schedule wild bird while it is on or near a nest containing eggs or unflown young, is also an offence. The fourth schedule identifies birds which may not be sold alive unless close-ringed and bred in captivity.

The Secretary of State has the power to amend all schedules and various provisions of the Act. Up-to-date details of the law relating to birds are obtainable in *Wild birds and the law* published by the Royal Society for the Protection of Birds (RSPB).

32. Mouse-eared bat (*Myotis myotis*)

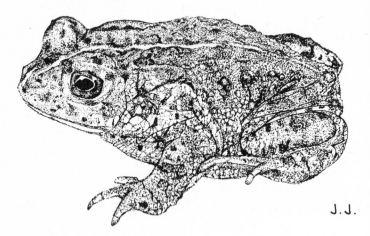

J.J.

33. English Natterjack toad (*Bufo calamita*)

The other legal protection afforded to rare and endangered species arises out of the **Conservation of Wild Creatures and Wild Plants Act** 1975, which amalgamates two Bills originally drawn up separately, one intended to protect animals and the other plants. This Act makes it illegal for any person, without reasonable excuse, to take, kill or injure any wild creatures on Schedule 1 to the Act, or attempt to do so. Nor may an unauthorized person sell a scheduled creature or have one in his possession. Species specifically covered at present on the first schedule are the greater horseshoe and mouse-eared bats (ill. 32); sand lizard; smooth snake and natterjack toad (ill. 33);

and the large blue butterfly. The eggs, larvae, and pupae of these wild creatures, where appropriate, are also protected. The Act also prohibits the marking and ringing of all species of bats—not just the rarer ones. The Secretary of State for the Environment can amend this schedule on the advice of the NCC; the first species to be added was the otter, from 1 January 1978 in England and Wales only; the Essex Emerald Moth was added in 1979. Section 7 of the Act enables species to be protected, among other things, by area and at particular times of the year.

Attempts to obtain legislation to cover plants had started over 50 years earlier: the Society for the Protection of Nature Reserves (now known as the Society for the Promotion of Nature Conservation) proposed the setting up of the Society for the Protection and Preservation of Wild Flowers in 1925 and sent out a leaflet to all county council's pressing for the enactment of a by-law. A by-law was passed soon afterwards with a fine for a first offence not exceeding £5. In 1933 the model by-law recommended by the Home Office was reframed to include primroses and read 'no person shall (without lawful authority) uproot, any ferns, primroses or other plant growing in any road, lane, roadside waste, roadside bank or hedge, common or other place to which the public has access'.

In 1934 and again in 1967 there was an attempt to obtain a Wild Plants Act; but this was not achieved until 1975. This Act makes it illegal for anyone to pick, uproot or destroy 21 listed endangered plant species which includes several orchids, alpine species and ferns (ills. 34–37). As usual several exceptions have been provided, the most notable being unavoidable damage by farmers and others to protected plants as a result of 'good agricultural or forestry practice'. This Act also makes it illegal for unauthorized persons to uproot wild plants, but it is important to emphasize that this general provision relates to uprooting and not to picking, so that the picking of blackberries or bluebells is not an offence whereas the digging up of primroses from the wild for cultivation in the garden, without specific permission from the landowner, is an offence. Both in the case of wild animals and plants, somebody who makes a genuine error of recognition is covered by the words 'reasonable excuse'. The NCC may grant licences under the Act in specific circumstances for educational, research or scientific purposes, or for collection.

34. Cheddar Pink (*Dianthus gratianopolitanus*)  35. Teesdale Sandwort (*Minuartia stricta*)

36. Tufted Saxifrage (*Saxifraga caespitosa*)  37. Killarney Fern (*Trichomanes speciosum*)

Under the **Theft Act** 1968, which does not apply to Scotland, plants are 'property' and it is, therefore, a general offence to steal a tree, plant or shrub. However, the Act goes out of its way to say that picking flowers, fruit or foliage from a plant growing in the wild does not constitute a theft unless it is being done for the purposes of sale, reward or other commercial purposes. Damage to trees and shrubs is covered by the **Criminal Damage Act** 1971. In addition, a local authority, with the approval of the appropriate Minister, can make a Tree Preservation Order (TPO) under the Town and Country Planning Acts, prohibiting the felling, lopping or destruction of trees without the consent of the local planning authority. However, the main problem with TPOs has been that the very low fine for not complying with them has been no deterrent. Injurious weeds are dealt with by the **Weeds Act** 1959, under which occupiers of land may be required to destroy spear and creeping thistle, curled and broad-leaved dock, ragwort, and such additional injurious weeds as may be prescribed by the Minister.

Until 1959 the only laws relating to wildlife, other than the Protection of Birds Act and a series of complicated game laws, were the Grey Seals Protection Acts of 1914 and 1932. The latter established close seasons from 1 September to 31 December. Earlier in this century the populations of grey seals were thought to be in danger in British waters; some naturalists estimated their number as low as 500 in 1914, but by 1970 the population had increased to about 37 000. Controversy raged over the decision to vary the close season in order to cull a certain number of grey seal pups each year. The problem brought about widespread discussion in Britain of some of the ideas underlying modern nature conservation and resulted in the **Conservation of Seals Act** in 1970. This Act defines the prohibited methods of killing seals—poisons and certain firearms—and continues the annual close season. In addition it makes provision for a close season for common seals from 1 June to 31 August. Orders can be made for protection in certain areas outside the close season. There are also the general exceptions for the taking of disabled seals and/or unavoidable killing as well as for the prevention of damage to fishing nets. Individuals can also be licensed for scientific or educational purposes, for taking for zoological gardens or collections, or for the prevention of damage to fisheries. The reduction of seal populations for management purposes, and the use of a population surplus of seals as a resource, is also allowed. The Conservation of Seals Act 1970 has helped to reduce excessive and inhumane slaughter but it is based on the sound conservation principle of maintaining populations at appropriate levels.

The **Deer (Scotland) Act** 1959 provides for the conservation and control of red deer in Scotland and allows the Secretary of State to make orders for close seasons for any species of deer. At present, red, fallow, and sika deer are protected by close seasons. The Act also makes it an offence to poach deer, or to use any method except shooting to kill them. In England and Wales the **Deer Act** 1963 provides close seasons for both sexes of red, fallow, sika and roe deer. Generally, deer may only be killed by shooting with a rifle of at least 0.240 calibre or shotguns not less than 12 bore. The use of spears, arrows or vehicles is forbidden. In recent years there have been several attempts to give greater protection to deer and close loopholes in the law which the Deer Society feel exist.

The other Act of Parliament concerning mammals is the **Badgers Act** passed in 1973 (ill. 38). This made it illegal for any person, other than an authorized person, wilfully to kill, injure or take any badger or to attempt to carry out these actions, and with certain exceptions possess a recently killed badger or a pelt from a freshly skinned badger. It also makes it an offence for anyone to ill-treat a badger or to use, with intent to kill or take a badger, badger tongs or any

38. Badger (*Meles meles*)

firearm other than a smooth bore weapon of a certain type. The Act also makes it illegal to offer for sale and, subject to certain conditions, to keep, ring, tag or otherwise mark a badger. Nobody may dig for badgers or, within an area of specified protection, kill or take badgers; however, those authorized persons and landowners who can satisfy the court before whom they are charged that their actions were necessary to prevent serious damage to land, crops, poultry or other forms of property, or to prevent the spread of disease—for example bovine tuberculosis—will not be guilty of an offence in this respect. The normal exceptions are made in the case of disabled animals and where licences have been obtained.

## 2. The protection of sites

The **National Parks and Access to the Countryside Act** 1949 and the more recent **Countryside Act** 1968 provided for the preservation and enhancement of natural beauty in the countryside, including matters relating to access, the setting up of special areas including the National Parks and the establishment of the Countryside Commission. National Parks, Country Parks and Areas of Outstanding Natural Beauty are not, however, nature reserves but attractive countryside where development is more closely controlled and where management is practised, including provision for appropriate outdoor recreation (ill. 39).

The 1949 Act, however, also created the Nature Conservancy with the function of establishing, maintaining and managing nature reserves in Great Britain—reserves that have come to be known as National Nature Reserves (NNRs). In 1973, the Nature Conservancy became the Nature Conservancy Council (NCC), under the Act of the same name. One of the major changes of this Act was the transfer of the research undertaken by the Nature Conservancy to the Natural Environment Research Council (NERC) where it is now carried out by the various research stations of the Institute of Terrestrial Ecology.

The first NNR to be established was Beinn Eighe in the Scottish Highlands—an area of 4 757 ha (11 757 acres), notable for its large remnant of Caledonian Pine Woods. In England, Scolt Head Island on the north coast of Norfolk was the first to be established, in March 1954. Today there are over 160 NNRs covering over

"AYE, IT'S A BEAUTIFUL BIT OF COUNTRYSIDE —
PEOPLE COME FROM MILES AROUND TO SPOIL IT!"

39. 'Aye, it's a beautiful bit of countryside – people come from miles around to spoil it'
(Rolf Whitworth)

126 000 ha which have been selected because they represent some of
the best examples of types of habitat in the country. In *A Nature
Conservation Review* edited by Derek Ratcliffe of the NCC, there is
an inventory of Grade 1 and 2 sites of scientific and wildlife interest
which the NCC regard as of major importance throughout the
United Kingdom. The criteria for selection is contained in Volume 1
of the publication, which took ten years to compile.

Not all the important sites are managed by the NCC; nor, even if
they were available, has the NCC at this moment sufficient money
or manpower to establish them as NNRs. Some of the remaining
highest graded sites of equivalent value to NNRs are owned or
managed by voluntary organizations such as the RSPB, the Society
for the Promotion of Nature Conservation and its associated Nature
Conservation Trusts, and the National Trust and National Trust for
Scotland. These sites will usually have been notified as Sites of
Special Scientific Interest (SSSIs) or in some cases as bird

sanctuaries. The NCC has the statutory duty to notify the existence of SSSIs to the local authority. If a planning application is received which is likely to affect the SSSI the local authority has a duty to consult the NCC and must take their advice into account when making a decision. SSSI designation therefore affords some measure of protection against damaging development but unfortunately, from a nature conservation point of view, agriculture and forestry are not controlled at present by planning law. Under Section 15 of the Countryside Act, the NCC may enter into an agreement with an owner and occupier to retain the interest of the SSSI and make such payments as may be specified in the agreement. Owners of land of outstanding scientific interest may be eligible for exemption from Capital Transfer Tax on the value of that land when it comes to be transferred either as a lifetime gift or bequest—a financial incentive made possible by the Finance Act 1976.

Local authorities were also given the powers under the 1949 Act to set up Local Nature Reserves (LNRs); and over 50 have been created since the first two were declared within a fortnight of each other in 1952, at Aberlady Bay in Scotland and Gibraltar Point in Lincolnshire. In general the response of local authorities to these provisions to help conserve wildlife and natural features locally has been disappointing. Both the NCC and local authorities may use compulsory purchase powers if necessary, and may impose local by-laws on acquired sites.

### 3. General provisions
The **Countryside Act** 1968, mentioned in section 2, contains potentially one of the most significant sections for nature conservation in any act. Section 11 states that *every* Minister, government department and public body 'in the exercise of their functions relating to land under any enactment . . . shall have regard to the desirability of conserving the natural beauty and amenity of the countryside'. Natural beauty of an area being interpreted as including references to the conservation of its flora, fauna and geological and physiographical features. The **Water Act** passed in 1973, which brought about the reorganization of the Water Industry, spells out this section in detail giving the ten authorities it created the duty 'to have regard to the desirability of conserving

flora and fauna and geological and physiographical features of special interest' and 'to take into account any effect which their proposals would have on such flora, fauna (or features).'

Seemingly unrelated legislation can have implications for the protection and conservation of wildlife. It is only possible to give a few further examples here. The **Control of Pollution Act** 1974, for example, contains sections which have significance for improving water quality and there are the laws relating to the avoidance of cruelty and the control of pest species, for example, the many Agriculture Acts, the **Protection of Animals Acts** 1911 and the **Animals (Cruel Poisons) Act** 1962.

Information on the law relating to the management of predatory mammals is contained in *Predatory mammals in Britain* available from CoEnCo. Such mammals include the badger, fox, hedgehog, mink, mole, otter, pine marten, polecat, stoat, weasel, wild cat, domestic cat gone wild, brown rat and red and grey squirrels. It is perhaps worth mentioning that the activities of naturalists in the countryside will be to some extent restricted by the law; for example the collection of specimens can no longer be practised in the manner of the past (see p. 63 Chapter 3).

Finally a word about enforcing the law. In practice, an individual would do best to inform the police or to seek the advice of an appropriate public or voluntary body; for example, a Regional Officer of the NCC or of the RSPB in case of offences under the Birds Acts; the Ramblers' Association in relation to public rights of way or access; the local Nature Conservation Trust on any wildlife conservation problem. These bodies will help with general advice on the law and, together with the police, in investigating suspected offences. If an individual believes that he or she has seen an offence committed it is important to remember the following: be sure that an offence has really been seen and has not just been imagined; involve the police as soon as possible and always refer to the Act in question before proceedings are taken.

### Codes for collecting

Botanical Society of the British Isles. 1977. *Code of conduct for the conservation of wild plants.*

British Bryological Society. 1978. *Code of conduct for the conservation of mosses and liverworts.*

Geologists' Association. Dr E. Robinson, Librarian, c/o Geology Department, University College London, Gower Street, London WC1E 6BT). 1978. *A code for geological fieldwork.*

Joint Committee for the Conservation of Insects (Dr M. G. Morris, JCCBI, Furzebrook Research Station, Wareham, Dorset BH20 5AS). 1973. *A code for insect collecting.*

Nature Conservancy Council. 1977. *The seashore and you. A code of behaviour for users of the shore and shallow seas.*

## Further reading

Anon, 1975. *Know your law; England, Wales, Scotland.* Rossett: WAGBI.

Anon. 1979. Trees and the law. *Handyman Which?* 464–5.

British Museum (Natural History) 1975. *Wildlife, the law and you.* (BM (NH) Publication No. 780.) London.

Cooper, J. E. & Eley, J. T. ed. 1979. *First Aid and care of wild birds.* Newton Abbot: David and Charles.

Cooper, M. E. 1977. *Birds of prey and the law.* Hungerford: The Hawk Trust.

Council for Nature 1975. *A law for wild plants.* (Information leaflet). London.

Council for Nature 1975. *Conservation of Wild Creatures and Wild Plants Act 1975.* (Information sheet no. 6.) London.

Council for Nature *et al* 1977. *Predatory mammals in Britain. A code of practice for their management.* 3rd. edn. London.

Ellis, E. A., Perring, F. & Randall, R. E. 1977. *Britain's rarest plants.* Norwich: Jarrold.

Fox, C. 1971. *The countryside and the law.* Newton Abbot: David and Charles.

Gilbert, O. L. 1975. *Wildlife conservation and lichens.* Exeter: Devon Trust for Nature Conservation.

McClintock, D., Perring, F. & Randall, R. E. 1977. *Picking wild flowers.* Norwich: Jarrold.

Perring, F. H. & Farrell, L. 1977. *British red data book 1: vascular plants.* Lincoln: Society for the Promotion of Nature Conservation.

Pollard, R. S. W. 1976. *Trees and the law*. Guildford: The Arboricultural Association.

Royal Society for the Protection of Birds: 1978 *Wild birds and the law*; 1979 *Air gun users beware*; 1979 *Bird photography and the law*; 1980 *Information about birds and the law*.

Stubbs, G. S. 1972. *Wildlife conservation and dead wood*. Exeter: Devon Trust for Nature Conservation.

Winsch, G. S. 1973. *Gun law*. 2nd edn. London: Shaw.

Winsch, G. S. 1978. *Animal law*. London: Shaw.

**Relevant Acts of Parliament**

The Animals (Cruel Poisons) Act 1962
The Badgers Act 1973
The Conservation of Seals Act 1970
The Conservation of Wild Creatures and Wild Plants Act 1975
The Control of Pollution Act 1974
The Countryside Act 1968
The Criminal Damage Act 1971
The Deer Acts 1959 and 1963
The Endangered Species (Import and Export) Act 1976
The National Parks and Access to the Countryside Act 1949
The Nature Conservancy Council Act 1973
The Protection of Animals Act 1911
The Protection of Birds Acts 1954–1967 as amended
The Theft Act 1968
The Water Act 1973
The Weeds Act 1959

All these Acts may be purchased from HMSO, PO Box 509, London SE1 or through any bookseller.

# 10. Natural history and wildlife conservation organizations

Melinda J. Appleby and Susan M. Joy

The growth of naturalists' societies, nature conservation trusts and other organizations concerned with natural history and wildlife has already been outlined in Chapter 1. This chapter is chiefly concerned with the work of these bodies from the point of view of the individual naturalist, especially the newcomer, who will sooner or later need to decide which he or she should join. The decision may not be easy owing to the considerable range of choice available; this reflects something of the complexity of the world of nature but is also a tribute to the knowledge, enthusiasm and persistence of naturalists in pursuing their various interests. No one should be put off by a high-sounding name or by a mistaken sense that the national societies are remote, aloof and uninterested in anyone outside a small circle of experts. Each has much to offer the individual and, on the other hand, is dependent for its progress on the support of an active body of members.

The organizations listed in this chapter can be classified in various ways. A broad distinction for example, can be made between those whose primary concern is to study and advance the knowledge of their subject and those who are more concerned with conservation. The Linnean Society, the oldest natural history society, is an example of the first: the Society for the Promotion of Nature Conservation, of the second. This distinction, however, reflects a difference of approach and emphasis rather than a strict limitation of their activities. Thus, though the Botanical Society of the British Isles is probably best known for its *Atlas of the British flora* and other publications on the distribution and taxonomy of British plants, it has found itself increasingly involved in questions of conservation where development has been proposed on locations of rare native plants and vegetation types. It is also now accepted that effective conservation depends on the interest and sympathetic understanding of the public—and not only those who call themselves naturalists. The pressure of events leads logically to the naturalist developing an interest in conservation and to the conservationist becoming an educationalist.

The following chapter has been divided into two main sections;

the voluntary sector and the government sector. A further
subdivision has been made into categories covering general
organizations; young people's organizations; organizations
specifically concerned with certain habitats and habitat studies;
botanical societies; zoological societies; and amenity organizations
concerned with preservation and access to the countryside. Details
of local natural history societies and groups may be obtained from
CoEnCo (p. 159) on receipt of a stamped addressed envelope.

## Voluntary bodies

*Organizations active in the general field of natural history
and/or wildlife conservation*

British Naturalists' Association
Mrs W. R. Pauline
'Auquhorthies'
London Road
Thatcham, Berkshire, RG13 4LP

Founded 1905 to bring naturalists into communication
for the study and conservation of nature. *Membership:*
2 300. *Activities:* local branches (20); lectures and
rambles; lending schemes for publications from all over
the world. *Publications: Countryside* and *Bulletin* (each
3 p.a.); booklets on specialist subjects (e.g. entomology,
algae, amphibians, reptiles and plant galls).

Council for Nature
(*see also* Council for Environmental Conservation
p. 159)

Founded in 1958 to act as the national representative
body of the voluntary natural history movement in the
United Kingdom, acting on behalf of naturalists and others to
further the study and conservation of nature (closed down
December 1979 and functions transferred to CoEnCo). Its role as a
forum and catalyst were the main activities together with the

provision of information.

*Membership*: constituents (12); affiliated societies, local and national groups and museums (300); associates (100) and subscribers (1 100). *Activities*: information service; conferences. *Publications*: include *habitat* (newsletter, 10 p.a.); information sheets; directories of films and lecturers.

Fauna and Flora Preservation Society
Zoological Gardens
Regent's Park
London NW1 4RY

Founded 1903 to safeguard wild animals from extermination by interesting the public and governments in their preservation in natural conditions; promoting the establishment of national parks and reserves; and the legal protection of wild animals. With its worldwide role it is largely concerned with overseas problems, but it is also active with regard to British fauna.*Membership*: 3 500; members; benefactors and life. *Activities*: meetings for films and lectures; overseas tours. *Publication: Oryx* (3 p.a.)

Field Studies Council
62 Wilson Street
London EC2A 2BU

Information Officer
Field Studies Council
Preston Montford
Montford Bridge
Shrewsbury SY4 1HW

Founded in 1943 to encourage every branch of fieldwork and research whose essential subject matter is out of doors. Nine residential field centres in England and Wales, with resident scientific staff and good laboratory and library facilities: Flatford Mill, Suffolk; Juniper Hall, Dorking, Surrey; Malham Tarn, Settle, Yorkshire; Preston Montford, Shropshire; Nettlecombe Court, Williton, Somerset; Slapton Ley, Devon; Dale Fort, Dyfed; Orielton, Dyfed; Rhyd-y-Crenau, Betws-y-Coed, Gwynedd. *Membership:* (open to anyone interested) 6 000; individual and corporate. *Activities:* numerous courses at each centre, March to October; programmes from Information Office. *Publication: Field studies* (1 p.a.)

Institute of Biology
41 Queen's Gate
London SW7 5HU

Founded in 1950 to advance the knowledge of biology and to promote the professional standing, efficiency and usefulness of biologists. *Membership:* (open to professional biologists): 11 000; fellow; member; associate member; licentiate; subscriber and student. *Activities:* meetings, nationally and in 17 branches; appointments register; register of consultants. *Publications:* include *Journal* (five p.a.); *Journal of biological education* (4 p.a.); symposium reports; 'Studies in Biology' (booklets); *Biology as a career.*

Linnean Society of London
Burlington House
Piccadilly, London W1V 0LQ

Founded in 1788 and named after the Swedish naturalist, Carl Linnaeus, the Linnean Society is the original biological society of Great Britain. Its purpose is 'the cultivation of the science of natural history in all its branches'. *Membership:* fellows UK *c.* 950 and overseas *c.* 550; associates ages 18–29 and student associates 16–24. *Activities:* meetings monthly October to June; library of 90 000 volumes; collections; library and manuscripts of Linnaeus; correspondence and manuscripts of other 18th and 19th century naturalists. *Publications*: include *Journals* (*Biological*) (8 p.a.); (*Zoological*) (12 p.a.); (*Botanical*) (8 p.a.); symposia reports and *Synopses of the British fauna* (all published by Academic Press for the Society).

National Trust for Places of Historic Interest or Natural Beauty
42 Queen Anne's Gate
London SW1H 9AS

Founded in 1895 for the permanent preservation for the benefit of the nation, of lands and buildings of beauty or historic interest, and as regards lands the preservation of their natural aspect, animal and plant life. *Membership*: 780 000. *Activities*: there is public access to all National Trust property, subject to the needs of farming and forestry (members have free admission where a charge is made; there is a reciprocal arrangement with the National Trust for Scotland, see below). *Publications*: *List of properties*; *Annual report*; *Newsletter* (2 p.a.); *The National Trust atlas*, and individual guide books to Trust properties; gift catalogue available from sales department.

National Trust for Scotland
5 Charlotte Square
Edinburgh EH2 4DU

Founded in 1931 to encourage the preservation of places of architectural or historic interest or natural beauty. *Membership*: 78 000; ordinary; family; life and 'double life'. *Activities*: members have free admission to all Trust properties and to those of the National Trust in England, Wales and Northern Ireland. *Publications*: *Year book* and *Newsletters* (3 p.a.).

School Natural Science Society
Miss J. J. Sellars
2 Bramley Mansions
Berrylands Road
Surbiton, Surrey, KT5 8QU

Founded 1903 as a national association concerned with
the study of natural history at all stages of education.
*Membership:* 1 500; members and student members.
*Activities:* meetings for lectures and demonstrations by
specialists in scientific subjects and educational
methods. *Publications: Natural science in schools* (3
p.a.); pamplets on various aspects of science and
teaching methods.

Scottish Field Studies Association
Forelands
18 Marketgate
Crail, Fife, KY10 3TL

Founded to encourage and assist field studies in
Scotland, to provide residential facilities and courses to
encourage the preservation of wildlife and the amenities
of the countryside. Residential centre at: Kindrogan
Field Centre, Enochdhu, Blairgowrie, Perthshire PH10 7PG.
*Membership:* 300. *Activities:* the centre provides one-
week courses on natural sciences with resident tutors;
parties with their own tutors also accepted; courses are
also held at centres of the Holiday Fellowship and
Scottish Marine Biological Association. *Publication:
Annual report.*

Scottish Wildlife Trust,
8 Dublin Street
Edinburgh EH1 3PP

*Primula scotica*

Founded in 1964 to safeguard habitats and wildlife
species, both plants and animals, in Scotland; to

manage habitats and species so as to maintain and
develop their variety and interest; to promote interest in
wildlife and the countryside. *Membership:* 7 000; life;
ordinary; associate (junior). *Activities:* Branches (11)
arrange meetings and excursions. *Publication: Scottish
wildlife* (3 p.a.).

Selborne Society
Mrs L. M. P. Small
13 Woodfield Crescent
Ealing, London W5 1PD

GILBERT WHITE

Founded in 1885 to discourage cruelty to wildlife and to
protect places of scientific and natural beauty. To
promote, especially among schoolchildren, the study of
natural history and to perpetuate the memory of
Gilbert White. *Membership:* 400. *Activities:* monthly
lectures during the winter; monthly field meetings for
both members and juniors at the Local Nature Reserve,
Perivale Wood, which the society owns; visits to places
of interest to naturalists; reference library of books by
and on Gilbert White. *Publication: Newsletter* (4 p.a.).

Society for the Promotion of Nature Conservation
The Green
Nettleham
Lincoln LN2 2NR

Founded in 1912 and incorporated by Royal Charter,
the SPNC promotes the conservation of nature and
educates the public in an understanding of nature, an
awareness of its value and the need for conservation.
The SPNC works primarily through its corporate
members who are the 42 Nature Conservation Trusts
established mainly on a county basis throughout Britain
and for whom it provides the benefits of association and
support at a national level. The SPNC owns several
nationally important reserves in Britain, most of which

are managed by the local Trusts, and also owns reserves
in the Falkland Islands and the Seychelles. Formerly
the Society for the Promotion of Nature Reserves, the
SPNC historically, was closely involved with much
pioneering conservation work in Britain and abroad
including the Nature Reserves Investigation
Committees, in the 1949 National Park legislation, the
formation of many of the Nature Conservation Trusts,
the Council for Nature and the International Union for
the Conservation of Nature. *Membership:* corporate
(associated trusts) 42; associates (trusts' members)
110 000 and individual ordinary members elected by
Council (subscriptions variable). *Publications:
Conservation review*; *Annual report*; posters; wallcharts,
information leaflets and booklets; gift catalogues
available from Sales Department. See also WATCH
p. 145.


World Wildlife Fund UK
Panda House
29 Greville Street
London EC1N 8AX

Founded in 1961 the WWF is an international fund-
raising organization for the conservation of the world's
wild animals, wild plants and wild places, and has
national branches in some 26 countries, including the
UK. One-third of the money raised by WWF UK is
spent on conservation projects at home, often through
other bodies such as the Nature Conservation Trusts.
*Membership:* WWF UK has a membership scheme
(individual and family) as well as a network of
voluntary supporters' groups. *Publication: World
wildlife news* (4 p.a. for members only). See also Wildlife
Youth Service, p. 146.

Zoological Photographic Club,
D. Platt Esq
Heathside
Tubney Nr Abingdon
Berkshire OX13 5QQ

Founded in 1899 to encourage the illustration and
study of a branch of zoology by photographic means.
*Membership:* limited to 40. *Activities:* postal portfolio
of members' photographs circulated monthly for
criticism.

*Young people's organizations*

British Trust for Conservation Volunteers
10–14 Duke Street
Reading
Berkshire RG1 4RU

Originally founded in 1959 as the National
Conservation Corps, as part of the Council for Nature,
the British Trust for Conservation Volunteers became a
separate body in 1970. Members of the national and
local conservation corps volunteer to undertake
conservation work in the countryside, on nature
reserves or private land, both at weekends and during
holiday periods. Regional offices at London; Bath;
Doncaster; Newcastle; Halesowen, West Midlands;
Cardiff; Chorley, Lancs and Doune, Perthshire.
*Membership:* over 3 000 plus members of over 100
local Corps. *Publications:* include *The conserver* (4
p.a.); *Summer task programme* (1 p.a.) and practical
conservation *Handbooks* (list on request).

WATCH
22 The Green
Nettleham
Lincoln LN2 2NR

Founded in 1972 WATCH is run by the WATCH Trust for Environmental Education Ltd, and sponsored by the *Sunday Times* and the Society for the Promotion of Nature Conservation, the national association of the nature conservation trusts. WATCH is for children and young teenagers up to the age of 14 who care about nature and the environment and gives members the chance to play a useful and active part in conservation as individuals, not just as part of a school or youth group. *Membership:* 10 000. *Activities:* through the link with the Nature Conservation Trusts members may take part in local meetings, excursions or events. Local projects are also organized. *Publications: Watchword* (3 p.a.) and educational packs. *WATCH Books* 1–4.

Wildlife Youth Service
Marston Court
98–106 Manor Road
Wallington
Surrey

Founded in 1963 for the express purpose of encouraging schoolchildren and young people from 5–18 to play a greater part in the conservation of nature. It encourages in its members a lifelong interest in wildlife, its study and conservation and enables young people to combine efforts with scientists and naturalists to preserve wildlife by participating in study projects and by raising funds to finance special conservation projects. *Membership:* 250 000; Field rangers (full membership); associates (observers and Panda Club) and school group scheme. *Activities:* annual holiday adventure camps; field study projects; nature trails; film shows and lectures on conservation. *Publications: Wildlife* (12 p.a.); posters; wallcharts; leaflets and newsletter service.

Young Ornithologists' Club
The Lodge
Sandy
Beds. SG19 2DL

Founded in 1965 YOC superseded the Junior Bird
Recorders' Club. It is organized by the Royal Society
for the Protection of Birds (see p. 156). YOC
encourages young people up to the age of 15 to take an
interest in birds and provides opportunities for fieldwork. *Membership:* 100 000; individual; family; group
members (minimum of 10). *Activities:* meetings; advice
on observing; holiday courses; field outings; projects;
competitions. *Publication: Bird life* (6 p.a.).

Young Zoologists' Club (XYZ Club)
The London Zoo
Regent's Park
London NW1 4RY

Founded in 1959 to increase an interest and knowledge
of all wildlife among young people. *Membership:*
individual and group (minimum of 20). *Activities:* Six
free tickets to London Zoo and Whipsnade;
information bureau on animal matters; during school
holidays, films, talks, discussions, conducted zoo tours,
and visits to other zoos; corporate membership for
schools, or groups, provides 10 copies of each issue of
*Zoo magazine*; 30 free tickets to London Zoo and
Whipsnade Park. *Publication: Zoo magazine* (3 p.a.).

*Organizations specially concerned with certain habitats
and habitat studies*

British Cave Research Association
Secretary: Ian Penney
9 Grandview Road
Thundersley
Essex SS7 3JZ

Founded in 1972 to amalgamate the Cave Research Group (founded in 1946) and the British Speleological Association (founded in 1933). *Membership:* 930; individual and corporate (clubs etc.). *Activities:* national conferences in September; symposium in March; winter and summer meetings; library of British and foreign books and periodicals available to members. *Publications: Transactions* and *Bulletin* (both 4 p.a.).

British Ecological Society
Harvest House
62 London Road
Reading
Berks. RG1 5AS

Founded in 1904 to encourage the study of ecology. *Membership:* 3 000; members may subscribe to one, two or three journals at varying subscriptions. *Activities:* meetings; symposia and workshops. *Publications: Journal of ecology* (3 p.a.); *Journal of applied ecology* (3 p.a.); *Journal of animal ecology* (3 p.a.); *Bulletin* (4 p.a.) and symposium volumes.

Freshwater Biological Association
The Ferry House
Far Sawrey
Ambleside
Cumbria LA22 0LP

Founded in 1929 for the study of all aspects of the biology, chemistry and physics of fresh waters. *Membership:* 1 850; ordinary; life and corporate (universities, schools, angling associations, water authorities, etc.) *Activities:* laboratory and hostel on the shores of Windermere with facilities for visiting scientists; library (100,000 items catalogued, open to members); river laboratory at East Stoke, Wareham,

Dorset with facilities for visiting scientists but no hostel (enquiries to officer in charge); annual scientific meeting in London. *Publications: Annual report; Scientific publications* (mostly identification keys and methods handbooks); occasional publications and reprints free (members only); list and membership details from the Librarian.

Marine Biological Association of the UK
The Laboratory
Citadel Hill
Plymouth
Devon PL1 2PB

Founded in 1884 to promote zoological and botanical research in marine science and to increase our knowledge and understanding of marine organisms. *Membership:* 1 600. *Activities:* accommodation, apparatus and equipment for research for all branches of marine science; ships; public aquarium. *Publications: Journal of the Marine Biological Association* (4 p.a.) and *Plymouth Marine Fauna.*

Scottish Marine Biological Association
Dunstaffnage Marine Research Laboratory
PO Box 3
Oban, Argyll PA34 4AD

Founded in 1894 to promote research and postgraduate training in marine biology. *Membership:* open to interested persons; learned societies; universities and public bodies. *Publications: Annual report.*

The Soil Association
Walnut Tree Manor
Haughley
Suffolk LP14 3RS

Founded in 1946 to promote a fuller understanding of
the vital relationship between soil, plant, animal and
man, the Association believes that these are parts of
one whole, and that nutrition derived from a balanced
living soil is the greatest single contribution to health
(wholeness). For this reason it encourages an ecological
approach and offers organic husbandry as a viable
alternative to modern intensive methods. *Membership:*
4 800 home and overseas, with 42 active groups in the
UK. *Main activities:* educational and the organization
of courses on organic husbandry for the public.
*Publications: The Soil Association quarterly review* and
practical booklets each dealing with a separate aspect of
organic husbandry.

*Botanical societies*

General

Botanical Society of the British Isles
c/o Department of Botany
British Museum (Natural History)
Cromwell Road,
London SW7 5BD

B.S.  B.I.

Founded in 1936 the BSBI is an association of amateur
and professional botanists whose common interest lies
in the study of British flowering plants and ferns.
*Membership:* 2 400; ordinary; family; junior;
subscribers—schools, colleges, public libraries,
museums, societies, etc. *Activities:* field meetings,
conferences, exhibitions and surveys; panel of referees
and specialists. *Publications: Watsonia* (2 p.a.); *BSBI
Abstracts* (1 p.a.); *BSBI News* (2 to 3 p.a.); conference
reports; handbooks, local floras, etc., list on request.

Botanical Society of Edinburgh
c/o Royal Botanic Garden
Inverleith Row,
Edinburgh EH3 5LR

Found in 1836 it is the national botanical society of
Scotland. *Membership:* 550; fellow; member; student;
school groups; lady member; life member. *Activities:*
indoor and field meetings, including joint meetings with
the Botanical Society of the British Isles; library;
advisory service; research symposia annually,
particularly to encourage young botanists. *Publications:*
*Transactions and proceedings* (1 p.a.) and *Contemporary
botanical thought* (a compilation of lectures).

Fungi

British Mycological Society
c/o Department of Plant Sciences
Wye College
Nr Ashford
Kent, TH25 5AH

Founded in 1896 to encourage the study of mycology in
all its branches. *Membership:* 1 400; full and associate.
*Activities:* meetings (papers) and forays. *Publications:*
*Transactions* (6 p.a.) and *Bulletin* (2 p.a.).

Lichens

British Lichen Society
c/o Department of Botany
British Museum (Natural History)
Cromwell Road
London SW7 5ED

Founded in 1958 to promote the study of all branches
of lichenology. *Membership:* 480; ordinary; junior

associate (under 21, or 25 if full-time student) and family. *Activities:* meetings, annual exhibition and lectures in London; field meetings in all parts of the British Isles; herbarium (specimens loaned); library (books and reprints loaned to members); specimens can be checked by referees. *Publications: The lichenologist* (3 p.a.) and *Bulletin* (2 p.a.).

## Mosses and liverworts

British Bryological Society
A. R. Perry, Department of Botany
National Museum of Wales
Cardiff CF1 3NP

Founded in 1896 to encourage the study of all branches of bryophytes especially in relation to those of the British Isles, their taxonomy, distribution and conservation. *Membership:* 450; ordinary and junior. *Activities:* library; herbarium (specimens loaned); assistance with identifications; assistance to beginners. *Publications: Bulletin* (2 p.a.), *Journal of bryology* (2 p.a.) and *Census catalogues.*

## Ferns

British Pteridological Society
A. R. Busby
42 Lewisham Road,
Smethwick, Warley
West Midlands, B66 2BS

Founded in 1891 to encourage the study and conservation of ferns and other pteridophytes, their taxonomy, distribution and ecology, and the collection and cultivation of the fern varieties. *Membership:* 550; subscribers; members and students. *Activities:* meetings; lectures; discussions; field meetings including two one-week excursions annually; reading circle; assistance with identification. *Publications: Fern gazette,* and *Bulletin* (both 1 p.a.).

*Zoological societies*

General

Zoological Society of London
Regent's Park
London NW1 4RY

Founded in 1826 to promote the advancement of zoology and animal physiology. *Membership:* 6 600; ordinary fellows; annual subscriptions; scientific fellows; associates. *Activities:* owns and administers the Zoological Gardens, Regent's Park and Whipsnade Zoological Park (203 ha) near Dunstable; scientific meetings; library for fellows and for associates by permission. *Publications: Journal of zoology* (12 p.a.), *Transactions; Zoological record; International zoo year book; Nomenclature zoologicus; Symposia* and *Guide.* (See also Young Zoologists' Club, p. 147).

Molluscs

Conchological Society of Great Britain and Ireland
Mrs E. B. Rands
51 Wychwood Avenue
Luton
Beds. LUZ 7HT

Founded in 1876 for the study of mollusca, marine and non-marine, British and foreign, living and fossil. Caters essentially for the amateur. Special attention is paid to the ecology and distribution of British Mollusca. *Membership:* 600; full members; family members; life members and subscribers. *Activities:*

meetings monthly from October to May at the British Museum (Natural History) and field meetings during the summer. *Publications: Journal of conchology* (approx. 2 p.a.); *Conchologists newsletter* (4 p.a.); *Papers for students; Concordance to the field card for British marine mollusca; Atlas of the non-marine mollusca of the British Isles* etc.

Insects

Amateur Entomologists' Society
P. A. Sokoloff Esq
4 Steep Close
Green Street
Orpington
Kent BR6 6DS

Founded in 1935 for the promotion and dissemination of entomological knowledge with special encourage-ment for younger and less experienced entomologists. *Membership:* 1 500; adult and junior. *Activities:* advisory panel for enquiries and identification. *Publications: Bulletin* (4 p.a.), exchange lists, handbooks on Lepidoptera, Beetles and Wasps etc.

International Bee Research Association
Hill House
Gerrards Cross
Bucks. SL9 ONR

Founded in 1949 to promote and co-ordinate research on bees, including their management, substances produced and used by them, and their pollinating activities. *Membership:* 1 500; subscription according to grade and journals required. *Activities:* biennial conference; library (includes 23 000 reprints); information service. *Publications: Bee world* (4 p.a.); *Apicultural abstracts* (4 p.a.); *Journal of apicultural research* (4 p.a.); books and pamphlets.

Amphibians and Reptiles

British Herpetological Society
P. A. W. Bennett Esq
45 Holdenhurst Avenue
Finchley
London N12 OJA

Founded in 1947 to promote the study of amphibians
and reptiles, especially the European species.
*Membership:* 500. *Activities:* meetings (9 p.a.) have
particular reference to practical vivaria keeping, and
library. *Publications: British journal of herpetology* plus
*Newsletter* (2 p.a.).

Birds

British Ornithologists' Union
c/o Zoological Society of London
Regent's Park
London NW1 4RY

Founded in 1858 for the advancement of the science of
ornithology. *Membership:* 1 800; ordinary and junior.
*Activities:* annual conference; annual scientific meeting;
members have access to the libraries of Edward Grey
Institute of Field Ornithology, Oxford and the Linnean
Society of London. *Publication: The ibis* (4 p.a.).

British Trust for Ornithology
Beech Grove
Tring
Herts. HP23 5NR

Founded in 1932 for the study of ornithology,
particularly by amateurs, and with special emphasis on
work in the field. *Membership:* 7 000; ordinary; junior
and school societies. *Activities:* annual 'bird watchers'

conference, many joint meetings with local
ornithological societies throughout Britain; postal
lending library for members and members also have
access to the library of Edward Grey Institute of Field
Ornithology, Oxford. *Publications:* include *Bird study*
(4 p.a.) and *BTO News*.

Royal Naval Bird Watching Society
Lieut E. S. W. MacLure
Hon. Secretary and Treasurer
Melrose
23 St Davids Road
Southsea
Hampshire PO5 1QH

Founded in 1946 to encourage and promote bird study
particularly bird watching at sea among its members.
*Membership:* 350; open to personnel serving or retired
in the Royal Navy, Royal Marines, Merchant Navy and
associate services, British Ocean Weather Ships, Fishing
Fleets and Oil Rigs; associate members (not entitled to
full membership), libraries and museums etc. may
receive the Society's publications on payment to cover
the cost. *Activities:* co-operates with the BTO, RSPB
and other ornithological bodies; library of photographs
and slides. *Publications: Sea swallow* (annual report);
news bulletins and standard report forms.

Royal Society for the Protection of Birds
The Lodge
Sandy
Bedfordshire SG19 2DL

Founded in 1889 for the protection of wild birds
especially of rare and interesting species, by developing
public interest through education, by maintaining bird
reserves and promoting research into their conservation.
Owns, leases or manages 75 reserves conserving

important habitats or protecting rare birds and seeks to ensure that conservation has a voice in planning matters and that the best areas of ornithological importance are safeguarded; it investigates pollution through schemes such as its beached bird survey and seeks reconciliation between the interests of farming and wildlife (the Farming and Wildlife Advisory Group has its adviser based at RSPB headquarters). *Membership:* over 250 000; fellow and member (special rates for those under 18). *Activities:* courses for teachers and other adults on birds; extensive lecture programmes for schools; film library; film shows; local meetings and annual RSPB members' conference; speakers available on a regional level. *Publications:* include *Birds* (4 p.a.); leaflets; wallcharts. List of educational leaflets, catalogue of sales goods and brochure of films for sale or hire available. See also Young Ornithologists Club p. 147.

Wildfowl Trust
Slimbridge
Glos. GL2 7BT

Founded in 1946 as a registered charity for the study and conservation of wildfowl and the promotion of knowledge and interest in wildfowl in particular and all wildlife in general. *Membership:* 14 500; ordinary; associate; junior and corporate. *Activities:* comprehensive collections of the world's wildfowl at Slimbridge; Martin Mere, Lancashire; Washington, Tyne and Wear; Arundel, Sussex; Peakirk, Cambridgeshire. Wildfowl refuges at Slimbridge, Martin Mere, Washington, Arundel, Welney (Norfolk) and Caerlaverock (mid-September to mid-May— entrance charge). Observation facilities for all; also by appointment at Slimbridge, skin collection, reference library and laboratory facilities for visiting scientists. Escorted tours by prior arrangement for school parties with films and laboratories at Slimbridge and Martin

Mere. *Publications: Wildfowl News* (2 p.a.) and
*Wildfowl World Magazine* (2 p.a.).

Mammals

Mammal Society
c/o Harvest House
62 London Road
Reading
Berkshire RG1 5AS

Founded in 1954 to promote the study of mammals by
collecting and disseminating information, organizing
co-operative field studies, and generally stimulating and
coordinating mammal studies. *Membership:* 850;
members; affiliated bodies; junior members and
students. *Activities:* annual conference and symposium;
bat ringing scheme; badger survey; collection of
distribution records of British mammals. *Publications:*
include *Mammal review* (4 p.a.), *Handbook of British
mammals* (second edition published by Blackwell),
wallcharts, notes and *Newsletter*.

British Deer Society
Riverside House
Heytesbury
Warminster, Wiltshire BA12 9HJ

Founded in 1963 for the study of deer; dissemination of
knowledge of deer for scientific and educational
purposes; advice on management and humane control;
establishment and maintenance of proper standards in
the pursuit and killing of deer. *Membership:* 2 500;
ordinary; youth to 21; professional; corporate and
overseas. *Activities:* six branches in Scotland, nine in
England; closely allied to the Irish Deer Society; wide
variety of field and indoor meetings of society and
branches. *Publication: Deer* (3 p.a.).

*Amenity organizations concerned with preservation and access to the countryside*

The Camping Club of Great Britain and Ireland Ltd
11 Lower Grosvenor Place
London SW1 0EY

Founded in 1901 to encourage all in a greater appreciation of the countryside and to promote physical health and education by spending as much time as possible in the open air by means of camping, caravanning and similar activities. *Membership:* 175 000; full and youth. *Activities:* weekly meetings under district association sponsorship, during six to seven month period. *Publications: Camping and caravanning* (12 p.a.); biennial handbook and sites list; site guides for France, Italy, Spain, Germany, Austria and Switzerland.

Commons, Open Spaces and Footpaths Preservation Society
25a Bell Street
Henley on Thames
Oxon. RG9 2BA

Founded in 1865 to preserve commons, public open spaces, footpaths and bridleways for public use. *Membership:* 2 600; individuals and local authorities. *Activities:* annual general meeting; periodic conferences; gives legal advice on preserving commons etc. *Publications:* include *Journal* (3 p.a.) and pamphlets.

Council for Environmental Conservation
Zoological Gardens, Regent's Park
London NW1 4RY

Founded in 1969, following 'The Countryside in 1970' series of conferences, CoEnCo is a national coalition of

UK non-governmental organizations (NGOs) focusing on major environmental issues. It is a central agency designed to promote action by NGOs and make representations to governmental and other bodies on their behalf. *Membership:* 30 member bodies. *Activities:* works principally through committees and working parties on water, pollution, energy, transport, opencast coal, wildlife and youth; from 1st January 1980 it has undertaken to perform the major functions of the **Council for Nature** which closed down on 31 December 1979 and these include the provision of an information service; the youth work and the continued publication of *habitat*. *Publications:* include *Annual report, Scar on the landscape? A report on opencast coal mining* and *Habitat guide to farmland*. List on request.

Council for the Protection of Rural England
4 Hobart Place
London SW1X 0HY

Founded in 1926 the CPRE is England's foremost independent body concerned with the protection of the rural landscape. Nationally, CPRE campaigns inside and outside Parliament in the cause of rural conservation. At county and district levels, CPRE county branches (of which there are more than forty) seek to influence planning and development control policies of public authorities and private developers in a similar direction. *Membership:* over 31 000 including 2 500 affiliated societies; funded entirely by voluntary contribution—central groups; life and branch subscriptions. *Activities:* annual general and other meetings and visits; slides, films, exhibition material and speakers available. *Publications:* include *Annual Report; Bulletin* (4 p.a.) to central group members and *Background*. List of other publications available on request.

Council for the Protection of Rural Wales
14 Broad Street
Welshpool
Powys SY21 7SD

Founded in 1928 to organize concerted action to secure
the protection and improvement of rural scenery and of
the amenities of the countryside and towns and villages
in Wales. CPRW also acts as a centre for furnishing or
procuring advice and information upon any matters
affecting such protection and improvement.
*Membership:* over 200 affiliated bodies; individual;
family and joint membership; junior (under 21);
corporate; schools (subscriptions vary according to
size); OAPs on application and life. *Publications: Annual
report* and *Newsletter* (3 p.a.).

The Ramblers' Association
1–5 Wandsworth Road
Lambeth
London SW8 2LJ

Founded as a federation of rambling clubs in 1905 and
known as the Ramblers' Association from 1935, its aim
is to encourage rambling and mountaineering, to foster
a greater knowledge, love and care of the countryside
and to work for the preservation of natural beauty, the
protection of footpaths and the provision of access to
open country. *Membership:* 30 000 individuals and 450
affiliated clubs; ordinary; joint (husband and wife)
junior and student; OAPs and life. *Activities:* the work
of the RA is carried out by voluntary workers in over
thirty areas and 140 local groups, and coordinated by a
small paid staff in the London office. Publications:
include *Rucksack* (3 p.a.); list on request.

Youth Hostels Association (England and Wales)
Trevelyan House
8 St Stephen's Hill
St Albans
Herts AL1 2DY

Founded in 1930 to help all, especially young people of
limited means, to a greater knowledge, love and care of
the countryside, particularly by providing hostels or
other simple accommodation for them in their travels.
*Membership:* over 270 000; young people (5 and under
16); juniors (16 and under 21); seniors (21 and over).
*Activities:* no national meetings but local groups meet
regularly. Over 260 hostels in England and Wales where
members can stay the night when exploring the
countryside; many are suitable for school journey
parties, 22 have special facilities for field studies.
*Publications: YHA handbook* (1 p.a.); *Youth Hostels for
school journey parties* and *Youth Hostels for field
studies.*

Scottish Youth Hostels Association
7 Glebe Crescent
Stirling FK8 2JA

Founded in 1931 to help all, but especially young
people of limited means living and working in industrial
and other areas, to know, use, and appreciate the
Scottish countryside and places of historical and
cultural interest in Scotland, and to promote their
health, recreation, and education particularly by
providing simple hostel accommodation for them in
their travels. *Membership:* 40 000; under 16; 16–20;
and 21 and over. *Activities:* maintains 78 hostels in
Scotland. *Publications:* include *Newsletter* (2 p.a.);
handbooks; guides and maps.

Youth Hostels Association of Northern Ireland
56 Bradbury Place
Belfast B77 1RU

Founded in 1931 to encourage a greater knowledge,
love and use of the countryside; to provide hostels or
other suitable accommodation for its members on their
travels and to take any action possible to preserve the
beauties of the countryside and to obtain or maintain
access and rights-of-way. *Membership:* 9 000; juniors
and seniors. *Activities:* maintains 12 hostels in
Northern Ireland. *Publication: Handbook* (1 p.a.).

## Statutory bodies

Forestry Commission
231 Corstorphine Road
Edinburgh EH12 7AT

Created in 1919 by an Act of Parliament to promote the
interest of forestry, the development of afforestation
and the production of timber in Great Britain. Facilities
for the public include access on foot, forest trails,
nature trails, information centres, some observation
huts and photographic hides, camp and caravan sites,
holiday houses, picnic places, arboreta and forest parks.
Details from the Forestry Commission. *Publications:*
include guides to Forest Parks and special forest areas;
leaflets on forestry wildlife obtainable from HMSO;
pamphlets on nature trails and forest walks available on
site; *Annual report.*

Countryside Commission*
John Dower House
Crescent Place
Cheltenham
Glos. GL50 3RA

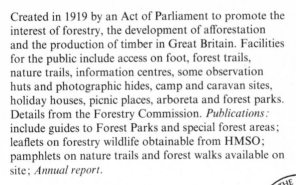

Created in 1949 by an Act of Parliament to select and designate in England and Wales National Parks and Areas of Outstanding Natural Beauty, to make reports to ministers proposing the establishment of long distance footpaths and bridleways, to provide information services relating to National Parks, to protect the Country Code, and to advise ministers and local planning authorities on questions concerning amenity anywhere in England and Wales. Information centres are provided by the National Park Authorities (a booklet giving details is available). Rights of access in National Parks are the same as in other parts of the countryside (see page 131). Most of the land is privately owned and visitors have no right of entry; the farmers' fields remain private inside National Parks just as they are elsewhere. Any additional access facilities to open country have to be specially negotiated by agreement with the owner of the land, or failing agreement, by what is called an access order. Publications list on request.

*Renamed from the National Parks Commission by the Countryside Act which came into force on 3 August 1968. The Act extends the Commission's powers and gives it country-wide functions, relating to the conservation and enjoyment of the countryside.

Countryside Commission for Scotland
Battleby
Redgorton
Perth PH1 3EW

Established in 1967 under the Countryside (Scotland) Act with duties to advise central and local government on matters relating to the conservation of the natural beauty and amenity of the countryside and the development of facilities for recreation and public access in the countryside. The commission is able to

provide grants to voluntary organizations and
individuals on projects designed to achieve the
commission's objectives. The commission may carry out
development projects at its own hand and has
developed particular interests in interpretation of the
countryside and in countryside education.

Nature Conservancy Council
19/20 Belgrave Square
London SW1X 8PY

Set up in 1973 by an Act of Parliament, the NCC is the
governmental body which promotes a national policy
for nature conservation in Great Britain. It replaced the
previous Nature Conservancy which was established in
1949 and which became a component body of the
Natural Environment Research Council (q.v.) in 1965.

The Nature Conservancy Council establishes and
manages some 160 National Nature Reserves (NNRs)
which cover almost 120 000 ha. The NCC's policy is to
allow as much public access to the NNRs as is
compatible with the primary aims of conservation and
research and acceptable to owners and occupiers with
whom it has nature reserve agreement (which apply to
over half the total area of NNRs); so there is free access
in some areas, and in others permits are required.

The NCC also gives advice about nature
conservation to Government Ministers, departments
and agencies, local authorities, voluntary bodies and to
individual land managers. The NCC has a statutory
duty to notify planning authorities and (in England and
Wales) water authorities of any area, other than a
nature reserve, which it considers to be of special
interest because of its flora, fauna or geological or
physiographical features. There are now over 3 600 of
these Sites of Special Scientific Interest (SSSIs); the
NCC has no rights over them but seeks to advise on
their conservation and management and may have to

present the case for safeguarding their interest at a public inquiry. The NCC also tries to show how the needs of nature conservation can be reconciled with other requirements in the planning and management of land and water generally.

The NCC seeks to foster an understanding of, and concern for, nature conservation. Its methods include interpretative work on NNRs; production of literature, exhibits and other materials; promotion through the press, radio and television; and collaboration with local education authorities and voluntary bodies.

The NCCs work is supported by research and survey, some of it commissioned from the Natural Environment Research Council, universities and elsewhere, and some carried out by its own staff.

Among other aspects of the NCC's activities are support for nature conservation internationally (for example through the International Union for Conservation of Nature and Natural Resources) and the issuing of licences and approvals to permit actions that would otherwise be illegal under protective wildlife legislation, for scientific, educational or conservation purposes (for example for ringing birds).

The NCC can make grants towards the costs of projects of any kind that it could itself undertake. In this way it encourages wider participation in the work of nature conservation and in particular supports the efforts of the voluntary bodies.

### Further reading

Civic Trust 1978. *Environmental Directory: national and regional organizations of interest to those concerned with amenity and the environment.* London, Civic Trust.

Department of Education and Science 1979. *The Environment; source of information for teachers.* London, Department of Education and Science.

# 11. Books and periodicals

David L. Hawksworth

There is a formidable and ever-growing literature on the world's fauna and flora which the amateur and professional alike find it difficult to keep abreast of, even in relatively specialized areas. In mycology alone, for example, about 1 500 books and articles concerning the identification and distribution of fungi now appear every year. Fortunately data from original research papers are eventually combined into definitive monographic treatments of particular groups. When this level of knowledge has been achieved field guides and other texts suited for general use can be prepared. Naturalists should appreciate, however, that a vast amount of specialist literature is available and is in a constant state of revision. Because the number of species in some groups is so large—particularly amongst the fungi and invertebrates—authors of guides have to be very selective about which species to include; consequently you should never assume that the organism you are trying to name is in the book that you have to hand on that group.

For many groups no field guides exist in any language, or do not exist in English. Where there are field guides in English—especially those illustrated in colour—the plates may originally have been published elsewhere in Europe and the text may be a translation from another language; you should use such works with caution as they may omit common British species and include others that are absent or rare in Britain.

The aim of a field guide is to enable the user to arrive at an identification as easily as possible (ill. 40). This can be done by lavish illustrations which can be quickly thumbed through, or by artificial keys. Keys are simply a matter of making the user answer questions in a yes/no manner in turn in a particular sequence; each choice eliminates one or more of the possibilities until a single name remains. An 'artificial' key is one designed to get to the right answer quickly rather than one which follows the classification hierarchy (a 'natural' key); an artificial key might emphasize 'petals blue versus yellow' as a choice, for example, whereas in a natural key the same groups might be separated on the basis of the arrangement of seeds in the ovaries.

40. Keying out a sedge in the field (photo: P. J. Shaw)

There are a large number of types of key available and many authors develop their own modifications to cater for particular groups. Fortunately most texts aimed at amateurs will explain in their introductions how they should be used. If you wish to learn more about keys, their construction and use, read the books by Davis and Heywood (1963), Hawksworth (1974) and Pankhurst (1978) (cited on p. 171).

The naturalist also needs to become familiar with the rudiments of scientific nomenclature. The internationally agreed rules controlling the applications of latinized names to organisms are termed Codes, but these are complex and difficult for the specialist, let alone the beginner, to understand fully. Fortunately an extremely lucid introduction to the various Codes of nomenclature is provided by Jeffrey (1977); after reading this, the reasons why some scientific names change, and differ from one book or periodical article to another, will be appreciated.

Latinized names should be learnt from the outset; many organisms have no English name, and others may have an English name which refers to more than one species. Scientific names are international and the key to the world's literature on the organism.

The identification aids that the naturalist will encounter first will probably be books or pamphlets. These are, however, very much the tip of the iceberg of the taxonomic (classification and identification) literature; as pointed out above, most of this is to be found in scientific periodicals. Some of the most useful periodicals for the amateur naturalist are listed on page 172. Many books can be borrowed from local public libraries, but more specialized works (including periodicals) may have to be obtained by your librarian through the inter-library loans service. Xerox copies of articles (subject to the law of copyright) can also be obtained directly from the library of the British Museum (Natural History), Cromwell Road, London SW7 5BD at a nominal charge per page.

The basic reference work to the literature for the identification of the British fauna and flora is *Key Works* (Kerrich *et al.*, 1978) which contains numerous references carefully selected by leading specialists on the various taxonomic groups (about 70 contributors were involved) and arranged systematically. This text should be available in the libraries of all centres where natural history is taken seriously, and the lists that follow (pages 172–190) are mainly selected from that compilation, supplemented by more recent publications. Works of particular value to beginners are prefixed by an asterisk (*). New books are reviewed in *Natural History Book Reviews, School Science Review*, and many other journals. New journal articles can be traced through bibliographic abstracting journals such as *Biological Abstracts*, but this is a very time consuming task; lists of the various abstracting services may be found in *Key Works* and in Bottle and Wyatt (1971). Bottle and Wyatt's book, although orientated towards bio-medical scientists, also contains useful information for teachers, sections on taxonomic and ecological literature, etc.

A special watch should also be kept on the series *Scientific Publications of the Freshwater Biological Association* and the Linnean Society's *Synopses of the British Fauna* (published by Academic Press). The first key produced under the national AIDGAP (Aids to the Identification of Difficult Groups of Animals and Plants) scheme was published in 1979 in *Field Studies*; these keys will also be available for separate sale and as they have been widely tested before publication by non-specialists they will be of particular value to the naturalist. Coloured photographs of a wide range of plants and animals are available cheaply in booklets of *The Jarrold Nature Series*.

## Sourcebooks

Bottle, R. T. & Wyatt, H. V. (eds.) 1971. *The use of biological literature*. 2nd edn. London: Butterworths.

Kerrich, G. J., Hawksworth, D. L. & Sims, R. W. (eds.) 1978. *Key works to the fauna and flora of the British Isles and northwestern Europe*. (Systematics Association Special Vol. 9.) London, New York & San Francisco: Academic Press.

## General

Cheatle, J. R. W. 1976. *A guide to the British landscape*. London: Collins.

Graf, J. 1958. *Animal life in Europe. The naturalist's reference book*. (English edn by P. Michael & M. Michael.) London & New York: Warne.

*Darlington, A. 1968. *The pocket encyclopaedia of plant galls in colour*. London: Blandford Press.

Hawksworth, D. L. (ed.) 1974. *The changing flora and fauna of Britain*. (Systematics Association Special Vol. 6.) London & New York: Academic Press.

*Lever, C. 1977. *The naturalized animals of the British Isles*. London: Hutchinson.

*Smith, K. P. & Whittaker, J. B. 1967. *A key to the major groups of British free-living terrestrial invertebrates*. Oxford & Edinburgh: Blackwell Scientific Publications.

*Southwood, T. R. E. 1963. *Life of the wayside and woodland*. London: Warne.

## Taxonomy & nomenclature

Davis, P. H. & Heywood, V. H. 1963. *Principles of angiosperm taxonomy*. Edinburgh & London: Oliver & Boyd.

Hawksworth, D. L. 1974. *Mycologist's handbook*. Kew: Commonwealth Mycological Institute.

*Heywood, V. H. 1977. *Plant Taxonomy*, 2nd edn. London: Arnold.

*Jeffrey, C. 1977. *Biological nomenclature*. 2nd edn. London: Arnold.

Pankhurst, R. J. 1978. *Biological identification*. London: Arnold.

Simpson, G. G. 1961. *Principles of animal taxonomy*. New York & London: Columbia University Press & Oxford University Press.

Stebbins, G. L. 1966. *Processes of organic evolution*. Englewood Cliffs, NJ: Prentice-Hall.

## Dictionaries

Abercrombie, M., Hickman, C. J. and Johnson, M. L. 1973. *A dictionary of biology*. 6th edition. Harmondsworth: Penguin Books.

Ainsworth, G. C. 1971. *Ainsworth & Bisby's dictionary of the fungi*. 6th edition. Kew: Commonwealth Mycological Institute.

Fitter, R. and Fitter, M. 1967. *The Penguin dictionary of British natural history*. Harmondsworth: Penguin Books.

Gray, P. 1961. *The encyclopedia of the biological sciences*. New York & London: Reinhold Publishing.

Gray, P. 1967. *The dictionary of the biological sciences*. New York, Amsterdam & London: Reinhold Publishing.

Grigson, G. 1974. *A dictionary of English plant names*. London: Allen Lane.

*Howes, F. N. 1974. *A dictionary of useful and everyday plants and their common names*. Cambridge: Cambridge University Press.

Kenneth, J. H. 1957. *A dictionary of scientific terms*. 6th edition. Edinburgh & London: Oliver & Boyd.

Stearn, W. T. 1973. *Botanical Latin*. 2nd edition. Newton Abbot: David & Charles.

Usher, G. 1974. *A dictionary of plants used by man*. London: Constable.

Willis, J. C. (revised H. K. Airy Shaw). 1973. *A dictionary of the flowering plants and ferns*. 8th edition. Cambridge: Cambridge University Press.

## Periodicals

Most scientific societies publish one or more periodicals (journals). The selection here emphasizes those likely to be of most value to amateur naturalists. A list of the specialist and other scientific societies in the British Isles is issued each year by the Biological Council in its *Calendar* (obtainable from: Institute of Biology, 41 Queen's Gate, London SW7) and this includes details of the journals issued and the addresses of the society's secretaries.

*Antenna*
*Birds*
*Bird Study*
*British Birds*
*British Phycological Journal*
*Bulletin of the Amateur
  Entomologists' Society*
*Bulletin of the British
  Mycological Society*
*Countryman*
*Countryside*
*Entomologist's Gazette*
*Entomologist's Monthly Magazine*

*Field Studies*
*Freshwater Biology*
*Journal of Bryology*
*Journal of Ecology*
*Journal of Zoology*
*Lichenologist*
*Magazine of Natural History*
*Natural History Book Reviews*
*Natural Science in Schools*
*Naturalist*
*Vole*
*Watsonia*
*Wildlife*

## Animal kingdom

*Protozoa*
Grell, K. G. 1973. *Protozoology*. Berlin: Springer.
Jahn, T. L. & Jahn, F. L. 1949. *How to know the Protozoa*. Dubuque, Iowa: Brown.
Johnson, L. P. 1956. Key to some common freshwater Protozoa. *Bios* **27**, 1–32.

*Porifera* (sponges)
Brien, P., Levi, C., Sara, M., Tuzet, O. & Vacelet, J. 1973. *Spongiaires. Anatomie. Physiologie, Systematique, Ecologie*. Paris: Masson & Cie.
Burton, M. 1963. *A revision of the classification of the calcareous sponges*. London: British Museum (Natural History).

Stephens, J. 1920. The fresh-water sponges of Ireland. *Proceedings of the Royal Irish Academy of Sciences* **35**, 205–54.

*Coelenterata* (polyps, medusae, sea anemones etc.)

Grayson, R. F. & Hayes, A. D. 1968. The British freshwater hydras. *Countryside* **20**, 539–46.

Hyman, L. 1940. *The invertebrates: Protozoa through Ctenophora.* New York & London: McGraw-Hill.

Kramp, P. L. 1961. Synopsis of the medusae of the world. *Journal of the Marine Biological Association of the UK* **40**, 1–469.

Russell, F. S. 1953, 1970. *The Medusae of the British Isles.* 2 vols. London: Cambridge University Press.

Stephenson, T. A. 1928, 1935. *British sea anemones.* 2 vols. London: Ray Society.

*Platyhelminthes* (flatworms)

Baylis, H. A. 1929. *A manual of helminthology.* London: Baillière Tindall.

Cox, F. E. G. 1971. Parasites of British amphibians. *Journal of Biological Education* **5**, 35–51.

Kennedy, C. R. 1974. A checklist of British and Irish freshwater fish parasites with notes on their distribution. *Journal of Fish Biology* **6**, 613–44.

Reynoldson, T. B. 1967. A key to the British species of freshwater triclads. *Scientific Publications of the Freshwater Biological Association* **23**, 1–28.

Wardle, R. A. & McLeod, S. A. 1952. *The zoology of tapeworms.* Minneapolis: University of Minnesota Press.

Young, J. O. 1970. British and Irish freshwater Microturbellaria: historical records, new records and a key for their identification. *Archiv für Hydrobiologie* **67**, 210–41.

*Nemertinea* (ribbon worms)

Gibson, R. 1972. *Nemerteans.* London: Hutchinson.

*Aschelminthes*

Rotifera (wheeled animacules)

Donner, J. 1966. *Rotifers.* London: Warne.

*Galliford, A. L. 1961–3. How to begin the study of rotifers. Parts 1–7. *Countryside*, n.s. **19**, 150–6, 188–94, 246–50, 291–4, 334–9, 382–8, 424–30.

Nematoda (roundworms)
Baylis, H. A. & Daubney, R. 1926. *A Synopsis of the families and genera of Nematoda*. London: British Museum (Natural History).
Filipjez, I. N. & Stekhoven, J. H. S. 1941. *A manual of agricultural helminthology*. Leiden: Brill.
Goodey, J. B., Franklin, M. T. & Hooper, D. J. 1965. *T. Goodey's The nematode parasites of plants catalogued under their hosts*. 3rd edn. Slough: Commonwealth Agricultural Bureaux.

*Acanthocephala* (thorny-headed worms)
Yamaguti, S. 1963. *Systema Helminthum*. Vol. 5, *Acanthicephala*. New York: Interscience.

*Priapulida* (proboscis worms)
Stephen, A. C. 1960. British echiurids (Echiuroidae), sipunculids (Sipunculoidea) and priapulids (Priapuloidea) with keys and notes for the identification of the species. *Synopses of the British Fauna* **12**, 1–27.

*Pogonophora* (beard worms)
Ivanov, A. V. 1963. *Pogonophora*. London: Academic Press.

*Sipuncula* (spoon worms)
Gibbs, P. E. 1977. British sipunculans. Keys and notes for the identification of the species. *Synopses of the British Fauna*, n.s. **12**, 1–35.

*Annelida* (true worms)
Brinkhurst, R. C. 1971. A guide for the identification of British aquatic Oligochaeta. *Scientific Publications of the Freshwater Biological Association* **22**, 1–55.
Clark, R. B. 1960. *The fauna of the Clyde Sea area. Polychaeta with keys to the British genera*. Millport: Scottish Marine Biological Association.

Fauchald, K. 1977. The polychaete worms, definitions and keys to the orders, families and genera. *Los Angeles County Museum of Natural History, Science Division Bulletin* **28**, 1–190.

Gerard, B. M. 1964. Lumbricidae (Annelida). *Synopses of the British Fauna* **6**, 1–36.

Mann, K. H. 1964. A key to the British freshwater leeches with notes on their ecology. *Scientific Publications of the Freshwater Biological Association* **14**, 1–50.

Mann, K. H. 1965. *Leeches (Hirudinea)*. London: Pergamon Press.

*Chelicerata* (Arachnida)

Araneae (spiders)

*Bristowe, W. S. 1971. *The world of spiders*. Rev. edn. London: Collins.

Locket, G. H., Millidge, A. F. & Merrett, P. 1951, 1953, 1974. *British spiders*. 3 vols. London: Ray Society.

Pseudoscorpiones (false scorpions)

Evans, G. O. & Browning, E. B. 1954. Pseudoscorpiones. *Synopses of the British Fauna* **10**, 1–23.

Opiliones (harvestmen)

Sankey, J. H. P. & Savory, T. H. 1974. British harvestmen. *Synopses of the British Fauna*, n.s. **4**, 1–76.

Acari (mites, ticks, etc.)

Arthur, D. R. 1963. *British ticks*. London: Butterworth.

Evans, G. O., Sheals, J. G. & Macfarlane, D. 1961. *The terrestrial Acari of the British Isles*. Vol. 1. London: British Museum (Natural History).

Hughes, A. M. 1976. The mites of stored food and houses. *Technical Bulletin of the Ministry of Agriculture, Fisheries & Food* **9**, 1–400.

Jeppson, L. R., Keifer, H. H. & Baker, E. W. 1975. *Mites injurious to economic plants*. Berkeley: University of California Press.

Soar, C. D. & Williamson, W. 1925–9. *The British Hydracarina*. 3 vols. London: Ray Society.

Pycnogonida (sea spiders)
King, P. E. 1974. British sea spiders. *Synopses of the British Fauna*, n.s. **5**, 1–68.

*Crustacea*
Branchiopoda
Scourfield, D. J. & Harding, J. P. 1958. A key to the British species of freshwater Cladocera with notes on their ecology. *Scientific Publications of the Freshwater Biological Association* **5**, 1–55.

Copepoda
Harding, J. H. & Smith, W. A. 1960. A key to the British freshwater cyclopid and canaloid copepods. *Scientific Publications of the Freshwater Biological Association* **18**, 1–54.
Kabata, Z. 1979. *Parasitic Copepoda of British fishes*. London: Ray Society.
Lang, K. 1948. *Monographie der Harpacticiden*. 2 vols. Lund: Ohlsson.

Cirripedia (barnacles)
Southward, A. J. 1976. On the taxonomic status and distribution of *Chthamalus stellatus* (Crustacea, Cirripedia) in the north-east Atlantic region; with a key to the common intertidal barnacles of Britain. *Journal of the Marine Biological Association of the UK* **56**, 1007–28.

Malacostraca (shrimps, crabs, woodlice, etc.)
Allen, J. A. 1967. *The fauna of the Clyde Sea area. Crustacea: Euphausiacea* and *Decapoda, with an illustrated key to the British species*. Millport: Scottish Marine Biological Association.
Gledhill, T., Sutcliffe, D. W. & Williams, W. D. 1976. A revised key to the British species of Crustacea: Malacostraca occurring in fresh water with notes on their ecology and distribution. *Scientific Publications of the Freshwater Biological Association* **32**, 1–72.
Harrison, R. J. 1944. Caprellidae (Amphipoda, Crustacea). *Synopses of the British Fauna*, **2**, 1–27.
Ingle, R. W. 1976. *A guide to the identification of British crabs (Decapoda, Brachyura)*. London: British Museum (Natural History).

Lincoln, R. J. 1979. *British Marine Amphipoda: Gammaridea.*
London: British Museum (Natural History).

Naylor, E. 1972. British marine isopods. *Synopses of the British Fauna*, n.s. **3**, 1–86.

Reid, D. M. 1944. Gammaridea (Amphipoda) with keys to the families of British Gammaridea. *Synopses of the British Fauna* **3**, 1–33.

Reid, D. M. 1947. Talitridae (Crustacea Amphipoda). *Synopses of the British Fauna* **7**, 1–25.

Smaldon, G. 1979. British coastal shrimps and prawns. *Synopses of the British Fauna*, n.s. **15**, 1–126.

Sutton, S. L. 1972. *Woodlice.* London: Ginn.

Tattersall, W. M. & Tattersall, O. S. 1951. *The British Mysidacea.* London: Ray Society.

*Uniramia*

Myriapoda (millipedes and centipedes)

Blower, J. G. 1958. British millipedes (Diplopoda). *Synopses of the British Fauna* **11**, 1–74.

Eason, E. H. 1964. *Centipedes of the British Isles.* London: Warne.

Symphyla

Edwards, C. A. 1959. A revision of the British Symphyla. *Proceedings of the Zoological Society of London* **132**, 403–39.

Hexapoda (Insects)

Alford, D. V. 1975. *Bumblebees.* London: Davis-Poynter.

Balfour-Browne, F. 1950, 1958. *British water beetles.* 3 vols. London: Ray Society.

Barnes, H. F. 1946–69. *Gall midges of economic importance.* 8 vols. London: Crosby Lockwood.

Blackman, R. 1975. *Aphids.* London: Ginn.

Bradley, J. D., Tremewan, W. G. & Smith, A. 1973. *British tortricoid moths.* London: Ray Society.

Brindle, A. 1977. British earwigs (Dermaptera). *Entomologist's Gazette* **28**, 29–37.

Campbell, J. A. & Pelham-Clinton, E. C. 1960. A taxonomic review of the British species of *Culicoides* Latreille (Diptera: Ceratopogonidae). *Proceedings of the Royal Society of Edinburgh*, B **67**, 181–302.

*Chinnery, M. 1973. *A field guide to the insects of Britain and N. Europe*. London: Collins.

Chvála, M., Lyneborg, L. & Mouch, J. 1972. *The horse flies of Europe* (Diptera: Tabanidae). Copenhagen: Entomological Society of Copenhagen.

Collin, J. E. 1961. *British flies*. Vol. 6, *Empididae*. Cambridge: Cambridge University Press.

Colyer, C. N. & Hammond, G. O. 1968. *Flies of the British Isles*. 2nd edn. London: Warne.

Davies, L. 1968. A key to the British species of Simuliidae (Diptera) in the larval, pupal and adult stages. *Scientific Publications of the Freshwater Biological Association* **24**, 1–126.

Day, C. 1948. *Keys to the British Tachinidae*. Arbroath: Buncle.

Disney, R. H. L. 1975. A key to British Dixidae. *Scientific Publications of the Freshwater Biological Association* **31**, 1–78.

Donisthorpe, H. St J. K. 1927. *British ants*. London: Routledge.

Duffey, E. A. J. 1953. *A monograph of the immature stages of British and imported timber beetles* (Cerambycidae). London: British Museum (Natural History).

Fonseca, E. C. M. d'A. 1965. A short key to the British Drosophilidae (Diptera) including a new species of *Amiota*. *Transactions of the Society for British Entomology* **16**, 233–44.

Hammond, C. O. 1977. *The dragonflies of Great Britain and Ireland*. London: Curwen Press.

*Heath, J. 1977. Looking at butterflies and moths. *Natural History Book Reviews* **2**, 2–7.

Heath, J. *et al.* 1976. *The moths and butterflies of Great Britain and Ireland*. Vol. 1, *Micropterigidae–Heleiozidae*. London: Curwen Press & Blackwell.

*Higgins, L. G. & Riley, N. D. 1970. *A field guide to the butterflies of Britain and Europe*. London: Collins.

Holland, D. G. 1972. A key to the larvae, pupae and adults of the British species of Elminthidae. *Scientific Publications of the Freshwater Biological Association* **26**, 1–58.

Howarth, T. G. 1973. *South's British butterflies*. London: Warne.

Hynes, H. B. N. 1967. A key to the adults and nymphs of the British stoneflies (Plecoptera), with notes on their ecology and distribution. 2nd edn. *Scientific Publications of the Freshwater Biological Association* **17**, 1–91.

*Imms, A. D. 1977. *A General Text-book of Entomology*. 11th edn. (rev. by O. W. Richard & R. G. Davies). London: Methuen.

Kimmins, D. E. 1962. Keys to the British species of aquatic Megaloptera and Neuroptera. 2nd edn. *Scientific Publications of the Freshwater Biological Association* **8**, 1–23.

Kimmins, D. E. 1972. A revised key to the adults of the British species of Ephemeroptera with notes on their ecology. Rev. edn. *Scientific Publications of the Freshwater Biological Association* **15**, 1–75.

Linssen, E. F. 1959. *Beetles of the British Isles*. 2 vols. London: Warne.

Macan, T. T. 1965. A revised key to the British water bugs (Hemiptera–Heteroptera) with notes on their ecology. *Scientific Publications of the Freshwater Biological Association* **16**, 1–77.

Macan, T. T. 1973. A key to the adults of the British Trichoptera. *Scientific Publications of the Freshwater Biological Association* **28**, 1–151.

Marshall, J. F. 1938. *The British mosquitoes*. London: British Museum (Natural History).

Mound, L. A. *et al.* 1976. Thysanoptera. *Handbook for the Identification of British Insects* **1**(11), 1–79.

New, T. R. 1974. Psocoptera. *Handbook for the Identification of British Insects* **1**(7), 1–102.

*Ragge, D. R. 1965. *Grasshoppers, crickets and cockroaches of the British Isles*. London & New York: Warne.

Richards, O. W. 1977. Hymenoptera. Introduction and keys to families. 2nd edn. *Handbook for the Identification of British Insects* **6**(1): 1–100.

South, R. 1941. *The moths of the British Isles*. New ed. (rev. by H. M. Edelsten, D. S. Fletcher & R. J. Collins). 2 vols. London: Warne.

Spradbery, J. P. 1973. *Wasps. An account of the biology and natural history of solitary and social wasps with particular reference to those of the British Isles*. London: Sidgwick & Jackson.

*Step, E. 1932. *Bees, wasps, ants and allied insects of the British Isles.* London & New York: Warne.

Williams, D. I. 1962. The British Pseudococcidae. *Bulletin of the British Museum (Natural History) Entomology* **12**(1), 1–79.


Tardigrada (water bears)

Morgan, C. I. & King, P. E. 1976. British tardigrades. *Synopses of the British Fauna*, n.s. **9**, 1–132.


Mollusca (snails, bivalves, squids etc.)

Camerson, R. A. D. & Redfern, M. 1976. British land snails. *Synopses of the British Fauna*, n.s. **6**, 1–64.

Chatfield, J. 1977. *Welsh seashells.* Cardiff: National Museum of Wales.

Ellis, A. E. 1969. *British snails.* 2nd edn. Oxford: Clarendon Press.

Ellis, A. E. 1978. British freshwater bivalve Mollusca. *Synopses of the British Fauna*, n.s. **11**, 1–110.

Hunnam, P. & Brown, G. 1975. Sublittoral nudibranch mollusca (sea slugs) in Pembrokeshire waters. *Field Studies* **4**, 131–59.

*Janus, H. 1965. *The young specialist looks at land and freshwater molluscs.* London: Burke Publishing.

Kerney, M. P. & Cameron, R. A. D. 1979. A field guide to the land snails of Britain and north-west Europe. London: Collins.

Macan, T. T. & Cooper, R. D. 1969. A key to the British fresh- and brackish-water gastropods with notes on their ecology. 3rd edn. *Scientific Publications of the Freshwater Biological Association* **13**, 1–46.

*McMillan, N. F. 1968. *British shells.* London: Warne.

Mathews, G. 1953. A key for use in the identification of British chitons. *Proceedings of the Malacological Society of London* **29**, 241–8.

Smith, S. M. 1979. British marine molluscs. *Natural History Book Reviews* **4**, 4–7.

Tebble, N. 1976. *British bivalve seashells. A handbook for identification.* 2nd edn. Edinburgh: HMSO.

Thompson, T. E. & Brown, G. H. 1976. British opisthobranch molluscs. *Synopses of the British Fauna*, n.s. **8**, 1–204.

Young, C. M. & Thompson, T. E. 1976. *Living marine molluscs.* London: Collins.

*Brachiopoda* (lamp shells)
Rudwick, M. J. S. 1970. *Living and fossil brachiopods.* London: Hutchinson.

Bryozoa (moss animals)
Hayward, P. J. & Ryland, J. S. 1979. British ascophoran bryozoans. *Synopses of the British Fauna,* n.s. **14**, 1–304.
Ryland, J. S. 1970. *Bryozoans.* London: Hutchinson.
*Ryland, J. S. 1974. A revised key for the identification of intertidal Bryozoa (Polyzoa). *Field Studies* **4**, 77–86.
Ryland, J. S. & Hayward, P. J. 1977. British anaxan bryozoans. *Synopses of the British Fauna,* n.s. **10**, 1–188.

*Phoronida*
Emig, C. C. 1979. British and other phoronids. *Synopses of the British Fauna,* n.s. **13**, 1–53.

*Echinodermata* (starfish, sea urchins, sea cucumbers etc.)
Mortenson, T. 1927. *Handbook of the echinoderms of the British Isles.* Oxford: Oxford University Press.

*Chordata*
Tunicata (sea squirts etc.)
Berrill, N. J. 1950. *The Tunicata, with an account of the British species.* London: Ray Society.
Millar, R. H. 1970. British ascidians. *Synopses of the British Fauna,* n.s. **1**, 1–88.

Vertebrata: Pisces (fish)
*Christensen, J. M. 1978. *Fishes of the British and Northern European seas.* Harmondsworth: Penguin Books.
Maitland, P. S. 1972. Key to British freshwater fishes. *Scientific Publications of the Freshwater Biological Association* **27**, 1–139.
*Maitland, P. S. 1977. *The Hamlyn guide to freshwater fishes of Britain and Europe.* London: Hamlyn.

Wheeler, A. 1969. *The fishes of the British Isles and north-west Europe*. London: Macmillan.

*Wheeler, A. 1977. Looking at fish. *Natural History Book Reviews* **2**, 99–107.


Vertebrata: Aves (birds)

*Bruun, B. & Singer, A. 1970. *The Hamlyn guide to birds of Britain and Europe*. London: Hamlyn.

Cramp, S., Bourne, W. R. P. & Saunders, D. 1974. *The seabirds of Britain and Ireland*. London: Collins.

*Harrison, C. 1975. *A field guide to the nests, eggs and nestlings of British and European birds*. London: Collins.

*Hayman, P. & Burton, P. 1976. *The birdlife of Britain*. London: Mitchell Beazley.

*Heinzel, H., Fitter, R. S. R. & Parslow, J. 1972. *The birds of Great Britain and Europe, with North Africa and the Middle East*. London: Collins.

Parslow, J. 1973. *Breeding birds of Britain and Ireland: a historical survey*. Berkhamstead: T. & A. D. Poyser.

*Peterson, R., Mountfort, G. & Hollom, P. A. D. 1954. *A Field Guide to the Birds of Britain and Europe*. London: Collins.

Sharrock, J. T. R. 1974. *Scarce migrant birds in Britain and Ireland*. Berkhamstead: T. & A. D. Poyser.

Sharrock, J. T. R. 1976. *The atlas of breeding birds in Britain and Ireland*. Tring: British Trust for Ornithology and Irish Wildbird Conservancy.

*Williamson, K. 1977. Looking at birds. *Natural History Book Reviews* **2**, 48–51.


Vertebrata: Mammalia

*Bang, P. & Dahlstrom, P. 1974. *Collins guide to animal tracks and signs*. London: Collins.

*Brink, F. H. van den. 1976. *A field guide to the mammals of Britain and Europe*. 4th edn. London: Collins.

*Corbet, G. B. 1976. *Finding and identifying mammals in Britain*. London: British Museum (Natural History).

Corbet, G. B. & Southern, H. N. (eds) 1977. *The handbook of British mammals*. 2nd edn. Oxford: Blackwell.

Fraser, F. C. 1976. *British whales, dolphins and porpoises*. London: British Museum (Natural History).

*Lever, G. 1977. *The naturalized animals of the British Isles*. London: Hutchinson.

*Ovenden, D. W. & Corbet, G. B. 1980. *The wild animals of Britain and Europe*. London: Collins.

Page, F. J. T. 1971. *Field guide to British deer*. Oxford: Blackwell.

Vertebrata: Amphibia and Reptilia

*Arnold, E. N., Burton, J. A. & Ovenden, D. 1978. *A field guide to the reptiles and amphibians of Britain and Europe*. London: Collins.

*Leutscher, A. (ed.) 1966. *The young specialist looks at reptiles and amphibians*. London: Burke Publishing.

Smith, M. A. 1973. *The British amphibians and reptiles*. 5th edn. London: Collins.

# Fungus Kingdom

*Fungi: General*

Ainsworth, G. C., Sparrow, F. K. & Sussman, A. S. (eds) 1973. *The Fungi. An advanced treatise*. Vols. 4A, 4B. London & New York: Academic Press.

von Arx, J. A. 1974. *The genera of Fungi sporulating in pure culture*. 2nd edn. Vaduz: J. Cramer.

Domsch, K. H. & Gams, W. 1972. *Fungi from agricultural soils*. (Engl. edn by H. J. Hudson). London: Longman.

Hawker, L. E. 1954. British hypogeous fungi. *Philosophical Transactions of the Royal Society* B **237**, 429–546.

*Hawksworth, D. L. 1974. *Mycologist's handbook*. Kew: Commonwealth Mycological Institute.

Holden, M. (ed.) 1975. Guide to the literature for the identification of British fungi. 3rd edn. *Bulletin of the British Mycological Society* **9**, 67–106.

Johnson, T. W. & Sparrow, F. K. 1961. *Fungi in oceans and estuaries*. Weinheim: J. Cramer.

Larone, D. H. 1976. *Medically important fungi*. Hagerstown, Maryland: Harper & Row.

*Richardson, M. J. & Watling, R. 1975. *Keys to fungi on dung*. 2nd edn. London: British Mycological Society.

Wheeler, B. E. J. 1969. *An introduction to plant diseases*. London: Wiley.

*Myxomycota* (slime moulds)

Karling, J. S. 1968. *The Plasmodiophorales*. 2nd edn. New York: Hafner.

Lister, G. 1925. *Monograph of the Mycetozoa*. 3rd edn. London: British Museum (Natural History).

Martin, G. W. & Alexopoulos, C. J. 1969. *The Myxomycetes*. Ames, Iowa: University of Iowa Press.

*Mitchell, D. W. 1978–79. A key to the corticolous Myxomycetes. Parts I–III, *Bulletin of the British Mycological Society* **12**, 18–42, 90–107; **13**, 42–60.

Nannenga-Bremekamp, N. E. 1974. *De Nederlandse Myxomyceten*. Zutphen: K.N.N.V.

Olive, L. S. 1975. *The mycetozoans*. New York & London: Academic Press.

*Mastigomycotina and Zygomycotina* (Phycomycetes)

Fitzpatrick, H. M. 1930. *The lower fungi, Phycomycetes*. New York & London: McGraw-Hill.

Sparrow, F. K. 1960. *Aquatic Phycomycetes*. 2nd edn. Ann Arbor: University of Michigan Press.

Zycha, H., Siepmann, R. & Linnemann, G. 1970. *Mucorales*. Lehre: J. Cramer.

*Ascomycotina* (Ascomycetes)

Non-lichenized

von Arx, J. A. & Müller, E. 1954. Die Gattungen der amerosporen Pyrenomyceten. *Beiträge zur Kryptogamenflora der Schweiz* **11**(1), 1–434.

von Arx, J. A. & Müller, E. 1975. A re-evaluation of the bitunicate ascomycetes with keys to families and genera. *Studies in Mycology, Baarn* **9**, 1–159.

Butterfill, G. 1969. *Keys to the genera of amerospored and didymospored Pyrenomycetes*. Kew: Commonwealth Mycological Institute.

*Dennis, R. W. G. 1978. *British Ascomycetes*. 2nd edition. Vaduz: J. Cramer.

Junell, L. 1967. Erysiphaceae of Sweden. *Symbolae Botanicae Upsalienses* **19**(1), 1–117.

Müller, E. & von Arx, J. A. 1962. Die Gattungen der didymosporen Pyrenomyceten. *Beiträge zur Kryptogamenflora der Schweiz* **11**(2), 1–922.

Munk, A. 1957. Danish Pyrenomycetes. *Dansk Botanisk Arkiv* **17**, 1–491.

Petch, T. 1938. British Hypocreales. *Transactions of the British Mycological Society* **21**, 243–305.


Lichenized (lichens)

*Alvin, K. L. 1977. *The observer's book of lichens*. 2nd edn. London: Warne.

Dahl, E. & Krog, H. 1973. *Macrolichens of Denmark, Finland, Norway and Sweden*. Oslo: Scandinavian University Books.

*Dobson, F. S. 1979. *Lichens—An illustrated guide*. Richmond: Richmond Publishing.

*Duncan, U. K. & James, P. W. 1970. *Introduction to British lichens*. Arbroath: Buncle.

Fletcher, A. 1975. Key for the identification of British marine and maritime lichens I–II. *Lichenologist* **7**, 1–52, 73–115.

Gams, H. 1967. *Kleine Kryptogamenflora*. Vol. 3, *Flechten (Lichenes)*. Jena: G. Fischer.

Hawksworth, D. L. 1970. Guide to the literature for the identification of British lichens. *Bulletin of the British Mycological Society* **4**, 73–95.

*Hawksworth, D. L. 1976. Looking at lichens. *Natural History Book Reviews* **1**, 8–15.

*Hawksworth, D. L. & Rose, F. 1976. *Lichens as pollution monitors*. London: Arnold.

Hawksworth, D. L. & Seaward, M. R. D. 1977. *Lichenology in the British Isles 1568–1975*. Richmond: Richmond Publishing.

James, P. W. 1970. The lichen flora of shaded acid rock crevices and overhangs in Britain. *Lichenologist* **4**, 309–322.

Poelt, J. 1969. *Bestimmungschlüssel europäischer Flechten*. 2nd edn. Lehre: J. Cramer.

Poelt, J. & Vězda, A. 1977. *Bestimmungschlüssel europäischer Flechten. Erganzungsheft I.* Vaduz: J. Cramer.

*Basidiomycotina* (Basidiomycetes)
Teliomycetes (rusts and smuts)
Ainsworth, G. C. & Sampson, K. 1950. *The British smut fungi.* Kew: Commonwealth Mycological Institute.
Wilson, M. & Henderson, D. M. 1966. *British rust fungi.* London: Cambridge University Press.

Hymenomycetes: Agaricales (mushrooms and toadstools)
Henderson, D. M., Orton, P. D. & Watling, R. 1968. *British fungus flora: Agarics and Boleti. Introduction.* Edinburgh: HMSO.
*Kibby, G. 1977. *The love of mushrooms and toadstools.* London: Octopus Books.
*Lange, M. & Hora, F. B. 1965. *Collins' guide to mushrooms and toadstools.* 2nd edn. London: Collins.
Largent, D. L., Thiers, H. D., Watling, R. & Stuntz, D. E. 1977. *How to identify mushrooms to genus I–IV.* Eureka, California: Mad River Press.
Ramsbottom, J. 1923. *A handbook of the larger British fungi.* London: British Museum (Natural History).
*Ramsbottom, J. 1953. *Mushrooms & Toadstools.* London: Collins.
*Rinaldi, A. & Tyndalo, V. 1974. *Mushrooms and other fungi.* London: Hamlyn.
*Southill, E. & Fairhurst, A. 1978. *The new field guide to fungi.* London: Michael Joseph.
Wakefield, E. M. & Dennis, R. W. G. 1950. *Common British Fungi.* London: Gawthorn.
*Watling, R. 1973. *Identification of the Larger Fungi.* Amersham: Hulton Educational.

Hymenomycetes: Aphyllophorales (bracket fungi, etc.)
Corner, E. J. H. 1950. *A monograph of Clavaria and allied genera.* London: Oxford University Press.
Eriksson, J. & Ryvarden, L. 1973–6. *The Corticiaceae of North Europe.* Vols. 2–4. Oslo: Fungiflora.

Maas Geesteranus, R. A. 1975. Die terrestrischen Stachelpilze Europas. *Verhandelingen der K. Akademie van Weterschappen naturk. ser.* 3, **65**, 1–127.

*Pegler, D. N. 1973. The polypores. *Bulletin of the British Mycological Society* 7 (Suppl.), 1–43.

Ryvarden, L. 1976. *The Polyporaceae of North Europe*. Vol. 1. Oslo: Fungiflora.


Gasteromycetes

*Demoulin, V. 1969. Les Gasteromycètes. *Naturalists Belges* **50**, 225–70.

Dissing, H. & Lange, M. 1961–2. The genus *Geastrum* in Denmark. *Botanisk Tidsskrift* **57**, 1–27; **58**, 64–7.

Eckblad, F.-E. 1955. The Gasteromycetes of Norway, the epigean genera. *Nytt Magazin for Botanikk* **4**, 19–86.


*Deuteromycotina* (Fungi imperfecti)

*Barnett, H. L. & Hunter, B. B. 1972. *Illustrated genera of imperfect fungi*. 3rd edn. Minneapolis: Burgess Publishing.

*Barron, G. L. 1968. *The genera of Hyphomycetes from soil*. Baltimore: Williams & Wilkins.

Ellis, M. B. 1971. *Dematiaceous Hyphomycetes*. Kew: Commonwealth Mycological Institute.

Ellis, M. B. 1976. *More dematiaceous Hyphomycetes*. Kew: Commonwealth Mycological Institute.

Grove, W. B. 1932, 1937. *British stem- and leaf-fungi (Coelomycetes)*. 2 vols. Cambridge: Cambridge University Press.

Ingold, C. T. 1975. Guide to aquatic Hyphomycetes. *Scientific Publications of the Freshwater Biological Association* **30**, 1–96.

Morgan-Jones, G., Nag-Raj, T. R. & Kendrick, W. B. 1972–5. *Icones Generum Coelomycetum I–VII*. Waterloo: University of Waterloo.

Morris, E. F. 1963. *Synnematous genera of the Fungi Imperfecti*. Macomb: Western Illinois University.

Subramanian, C. V. 1972. *Hyphomycetes*. New Delhi: Indian Council for Agricultural Research.

## Plant Kingdom

*Algae*

Allen, C. O. 1950. *British Stoneworts (Charophyta)*. Arbroath: Buncle.

*Belcher, J. H. & Swale, E. M. F. 1976. *A beginner's guide to freshwater Algae*. London: HMSO.

Dixon, P. W. & Irvine, L. M. 1977. *The seaweeds of the British Isles.* Vol. 1: *Rhodophyta. Part 1. Introduction, Nemaliales, Gigartinales.* London: British Museum (Natural History).

George, E. A. 1976. A guide to algal keys (excluding seaweeds). *British Phycological Journal* **11**, 49–55.

Hendey, N. I. 1964. *An introductory account of the smaller Algae of British coastal waters*. Part 5, *Bacillariophyceae (Diatoms).* London: HMSO.

*Hiscock, S. 1979. A field key to the British brown seaweeds (Phaeophyta). *Field Studies* **5**, 1–44.

*Jones, W. W. 1962. A key to the genera of the British seaweeds. *Field Studies* **1**(4), 1–32.

Newton, L. 1931. *A handbook of British seaweeds*. London: British Museum (Natural History).

*Price, J. M. 1978. Seaweeds on shore: data sources for Britain. *Natural History Book Reviews* **3**, 3–13.

West, W., West, G. S. & Carter, N. 1904–23. *A monograph of the British Desmidiaceae*. 5 vols. London: Ray Society.


*Bryophyta* (mosses and liverworts)

Arnell, S. 1956. *Illustrated moss flora of Fennoscandia. I: Hepaticae.* Lund: Gleerups.

Dixon, H. N. 1924. *The student's handbook of British Mosses*. 3rd edn. Eastbourne: Sumfield.

Gams, H. 1973. *Kleine Kryptogamenflora*. Vol. 4: *Die Moos- und Farnpflanzen.* 5th edn. Jena: G. Fischer.

*Jewell, A. L. 1955. *The observer's book of mosses and liverworts.* London & New York: Warne.

MacVicar, S. M. 1926. *The student's handbook of British hepatics*. 2nd edn. Eastbourne: Sumfield.

Nyholm, E. 1954–69. *Illustrated moss flora of Fennoscandia. II. Musci.* 6 parts. Lund: Gleerups.

Smith, A. J. E. 1978. *The moss flora of Britain and Ireland.*
Cambridge: Cambridge University Press.

*Watson, E. V. 1968. *British mosses and liverworts.* 2nd edn. London:
Cambridge University Press.

*Watson, N. 1947. *Woodland mosses.* (Forestry Commission
Booklet No. 1). London: HMSO.

*Pteridophyta* (ferns and fern allies) *see also under* Spermatophyta

Hyde, H. A., Wade, A. E. & Harrison, S. G. 1969. *Welsh Ferns,
Clubmosses, quillworts and horsetails.* 5th edn. Cardiff: National
Museum of Wales.

Jermy, A. C., Arnold, H. R., Farrell, L. & Perring, F. H. 1978. *Atlas
of ferns of the British Isles.* London: Botanical Society of the
British Isles.

*Spermatophyta* (flowering plants and conifers)
General works

Butcher, R. W. 1961. *A new illustrated British flora.* 2 vols. London:
Hill.

Clapham, A. R., Tutin, T. G. & Warburg, E. F. 1962. *Flora of the
British Isles.* 2nd edn. Cambridge: Cambridge University Press.

*Clapham, A. R., Tutin, T. G. & Warburg, E. F. 1968. *Excursion
flora of the British Isles.* 2nd edn. Cambridge: Cambridge
University Press.

Davis, P. H. & Cullen, J. 1965. *The identification of flowering plant
families.* Edinburgh & London; Oliver & Boyd.

*Fitter, A. 1978. *An atlas of the wild flowers of Britain and Northern
Europe.* London: Collins.

*Fitter, R., Fitter, A. & Blamey, M. 1974. *The Wild Flowers of
Britain and Northern Europe.* 2nd edn. London: Collins.

Kent, D. H. 1967. *Index to botanical monographs and taxonomic
papers relating to phanerogams and vascular cryptogams found
growing wild in the British Isles.* London & New York: Academic
Press.

*McClintock, D. & Fitter, R. S. R. 1956. *The pocket guide to wild
flowers.* London: Collins.

*Martin, W. K. 1969. *The concise British flora in colour.* 2nd edn.
(rev. by D. H. Kent). London: Ebury Press & Michael Joseph.

*Nicholson, B. E., Ary, S. & Gregory, M. 1960. *The Oxford Book of Wild Flowers*. Pocket edn. London: Oxford University Press.

Perring, F. H. & Sell, P. D. 1968. *Atlas of the British Flora. Critical Supplement*. London: Nelson.

Perring, F. H. & Walters, S. M. (eds) 1976. *Atlas of the British flora*. 2nd edn. Wakefield: EP Publishing.

*Phillips, R. 1977. *Wild flowers of Britain*. London: Pan Books.

Ross-Craig, S. 1948–74. *Drawings of British Plants*. 32 vols. London: Bell.

Tutin, T. G. *et al.* (eds) 1964–80. *Flora Europaea*. 5 vols. London: Cambridge University Press.

Webb, D. A. 1977. *An Irish flora*. 6th edn. Dundalk: Dundalgan Press.


Specialized works

Haslam, S. M. 1978. *River Plants*. London: Cambridge University Press.

*Haslam, S. M., Sinker, C. A. & Wolseley, P. O. 1975. British water plants. *Field Studies* **4**, 243–351.

*Hubbard, C. E. 1968. *Grasses: A guide to their structure, identification, uses, and distribution in the British Isles*. 2nd ed. Harmondsworth: Penguin.

*Jermy, A. C. & Tutin, T. G. 1968. *British sedges. A handbook to the species of Carex found growing in the British Isles*. London: Botanical Society of the British Isles.

*Mitchell, A. 1974. *A field guide to the trees of Britain and Northern Europe*. London: Collins.

*Nicholson, B. E. & Clapham, A. R. 1975. *The Oxford book of trees*. London: Oxford University Press.

*Polunin, O. 1976. *Trees and Bushes of Europe*. London: Oxford University Press.

*Rose, F. 1965. *The observer's book of grasses, sedges and rushes*. London: Warne.

Stace, C. A. (ed.) 1975. *Hybridization and the flora of the British Isles*. London, New York & San Francisco: Academic Press.

*Summerhayes, V. S. 1968. *Wild Orchids of Britain, with a key to the species*. 2nd edn. London: Collins

*Turner Ettlinger, D. M. 1976. *British and Irish Orchids. A Field Guide*. London & Basingstoke: Macmillan Press.

*Williams, J. G., Williams, A. A. & Arnott, N. 1978. *A field guide to the orchids of Britain and Europe*. London: Collins.

# Appendix A

**Vice-counties**

The vice-county system of natural history recording in Britain (ill. 41) was devised by H. C. Watson (1804–1881) and a comparable system was produced for Ireland by R. Ll. Praeger (1865–1953). It has been employed extensively by botanists, and to a lesser extent by zoologists. Recording on a grid square basis (see p. 82) is now the method most widely used by naturalists; in local floras and faunal distribution studies this is usually employed within particular vice-counties. Lists of new vice-county records are a feature of most local, and many national, natural history society publications.

In determining to which vice-county a particular locality belongs, the gazetteers published by Bartholomew and the Ordnance Survey should be used in conjunction with the maps from J. E. Dandy's *Watsonian vice-counties of Great Britain* (1969, London: Ray Society), M. J. P. Scannell and D. M. Synnott's *Census catalogue of the flora of Ireland* (1972, Dublin: Irish Government Publication), and the Ordnance Survey maps (various scales) for Britain and Ireland.

ENGLAND AND WALES

1. West Cornwall (with Scilly)
2. East Cornwall
3. South Devon
4. North Devon
5. South Somerset
6. North Somerset
7. North Wiltshire
8. South Wiltshire
9. Dorset
10. Isle of Wight
11. South Hampshire
12. North Hampshire
13. West Sussex
14. East Sussex
15. East Kent
16. West Kent
17. Surrey
18. South Essex
19. North Essex
20. Hertfordshire
21. Middlesex
22. Berkshire
23. Oxfordshire
24. Buckinghamshire
25. East Suffolk
26. West Suffolk
27. East Norfolk
28. West Norfolk
29. Cambridgeshire
30. Bedfordshire
31. Huntingdonshire
32. Northamptonshire
33. East Gloucestershire
34. West Gloucestershire

35. Monmouthshire
36. Herefordshire
37. Worcestershire
38. Warwickshire
39. Staffordshire
40. Shropshire (Salop)
41. Glamorgan
42. Breconshire
43. Radnorshire
44. Carmarthenshire
45. Pembrokeshire
46. Cardiganshire
47. Montgomeryshire
48. Merionethshire
49. Caernarvonshire
50. Denbighshire
51. Flintshire
52. Anglesey
53. South Lincolnshire
54. North Lincolnshire
55. Leicestershire (with Rutland)
56. Nottinghamshire
57. Derbyshire
58. Cheshire
59. South Lancashire
60. West Lancashire
61. South-east Yorkshire
62. North-east Yorkshire
63. South-west Yorkshire
64. Mid-west Yorkshire
65. North-west Yorkshire
66. Durham
67. South Northumberland
68. North Northumberland (Cheviot)
69. Westmorland with North Lancashire
70. Cumberland
71. Isle of Man

SCOTLAND

72. Dumfriesshire
73. Kirkcudbrightshire
74. Wigtownshire
75. Ayrshire
76. Renfrewshire
77. Lanarkshire
78. Peebleshire
79. Selkirkshire
80. Roxburghshire
81. Berwickshire
82. East Lothian (Haddington)
83. Midlothian (Edinburgh)
84. West Lothian (Linlithgow)
85. Fifeshire (with Kinross)
86. Stirlingshire
87. West Perthshire (with Clackmannan)
88. Mid Perthshire
89. East Perthshire
90. Angus (Forfar)
91. Kincardineshire
92. South Aberdeenshire
93. North Aberdeenshire
94. Banffshire
95. Moray (Elgin)
96. East Inverness-shire (with Nairn)

 97.  West Inverness-shire
 98.  Argyll Main
 99.  Dunbartonshire
100.  Clyde Isles
101.  Kintyre
102.  South Ebudes
103.  Mid Ebudes
104.  North Ebudes
105.  West Ross

106.  East Ross
107.  East Sutherland
108.  West Sutherland
109.  Caithness
110.  Outer Hebrides
111.  Orkney Islands
112.  Shetland Islands (Zetland)
113.  Channel Islands

IRELAND

H.1.   South Kerry
H.2.   North Kerry
H.3.   West Cork
H.4.   Mid Cork
H.5.   East Cork
H.6.   Waterford
H.7.   South Tipperary
H.8.   Limerick
H.9.   Clare
H.10.  North Tipperary
H.11.  Kilkenny
H.12.  Wexford
H.13.  Carlow
H.14.  Leix (Queen's County)
H.15.  South-east Galway
H.16.  West Galway
H.17.  North-east Galway
H.18.  Offaly (King's County)
H.19.  Kildare
H.20.  Wicklow

H.21.  Dublin
H.22.  Meath
H.23.  West Meath
H.24.  Longford
H.25.  Roscommon
H.26.  East Mayo
H.27.  West Mayo
H.28.  Sligo
H.29.  Leitrim
H.30.  Cavan
H.31.  Louth
H.32.  Monaghan
H.33.  Fermanagh
H.34.  East Donegal
H.35.  West Donegal
H.36.  Tyrone
H.37.  Armagh
H.38.  Down
H.39.  Antrim
H.40.  Londonderry

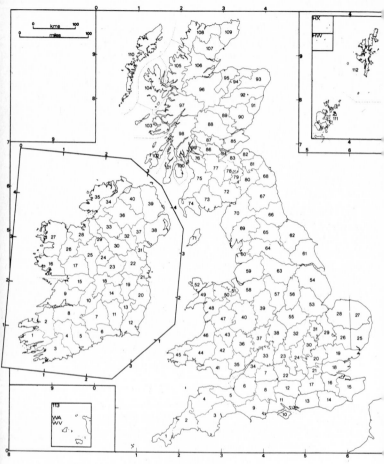

41. The Watsonian vice-county system of natural history recording

# Appendix B

**Grid references**

The National Grid of the Ordnance Survey is a system of reference for Britain. The country is divided initially into 100 km squares which are given a letter designation; earlier maps used a numerical system—this is still used by the Biological Records Centre (see p. 80) as it simplifies machine coding. The letter designations and numerical equivalents are provided in ill. 42.

Each of the 100 km squares is sub-divided into a hundred 10 km squares, which are sub-divided into 1 km squares on modern Ordnance Survey maps. The 10 km squares are also marked on the maps in the *Readers Digest AA Book of the Road*, the AA Roadbooks of England, Wales and Scotland, and recent editions of the *AA Members Handbook*.

To arrive at the grid reference to a 100 km square, read the number of the line forming the western boundary (this number is at the top and bottom margins of the map), and then the number of the line forming the southern boundary (this number is on the sides of the map). These two numbers *in the order given above* form the 100 km square grid reference to the square to the north-east of the point of the intersection of the two lines. The 100 km square is always quoted first and often separated from the rest of the reference by an oblique stroke.

The boundaries of each of the 10 km squares in a 100 km square are numbered in the same way and the grid references to them are arrived at by reading the numbers of the lines forming the western and southern boundaries of the square. The numbering of the boundaries of the 1 km squares in a 10 km square is on a modified system, but the grid references to them are arrived at in the same way. Where a more precise reference is required, the 1 km square can be further sub-divided into tens by eye or by reference to unnumbered divisions at the margin of the map.

Further details of the National Grid and how to arrive at a grid reference are given on all 1:50 000 Ordnance Survey maps.

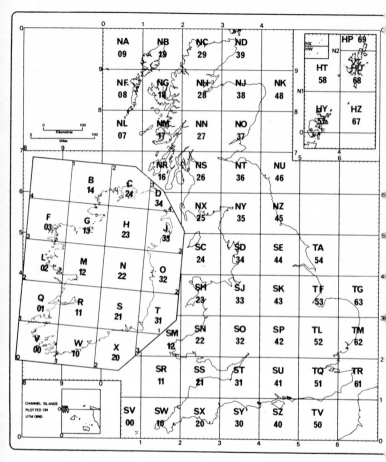

42. Numerical equivalents of the 100 km square reference letters of the National and Irish grids

# Index